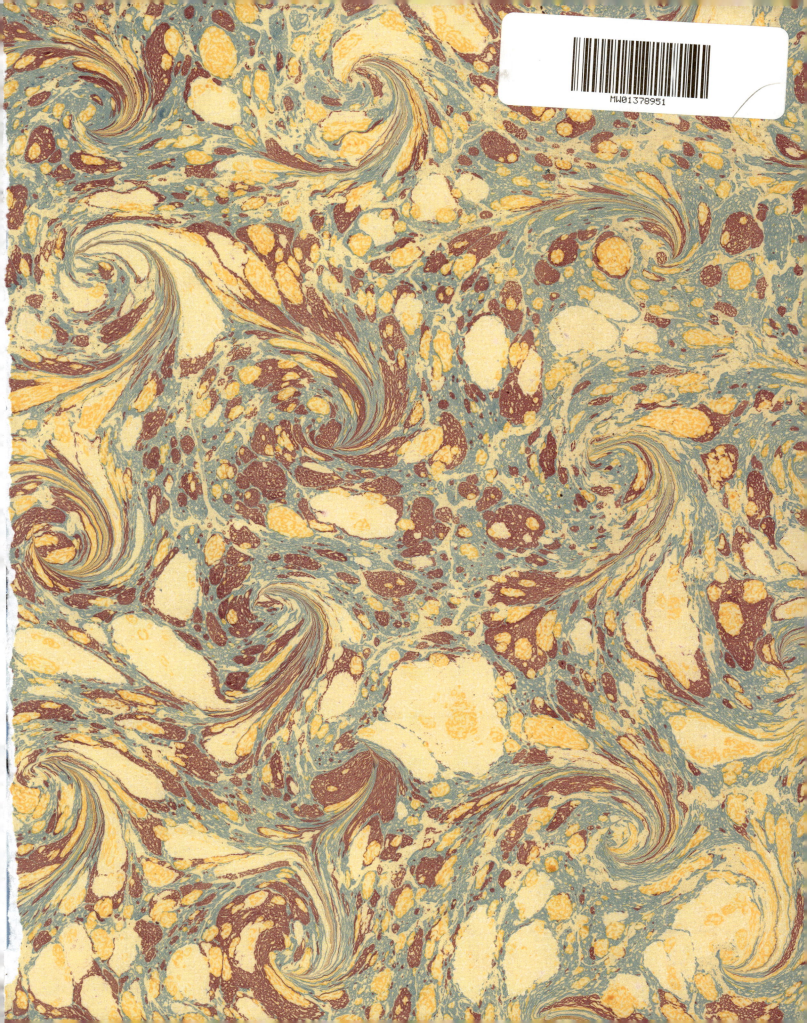

VOUGHT F7U CUTLASS

A Developmental History

Acknowledgments

I would like to take this opportunity to thank the following people for their tireless contributions to the completion of this book.Tom Cathcart whose "Top Gun" attitude and demeanor lay ed inroads of contribution in this overall effort. Dick Atkins and Joe Angelone true American Hero's in their own rite whose singular purpose lied in the acquisition of valued information from the archives and personal experiences at Vought Aircraft. Curt Lawson, the late Bill Hardman and the staff at the National Naval Aviation Museum located in Pensecola Florida,Tom Quinlan Director of The Pax River Museum, Jack Connors From Prat&Whitney, Janet Koonce from City Blue Technologies, Bill Spidel and my daughter Anna Gardner for her Impeccable patience and typing skills orchestrating the completion of this work. Lastly to my wife Susan for her constant and uncompromising encouragement through this endeavor.

Book Design by Bruce Waters

Copyright © 2010 by Tom Gardner
Library of Congress Control Number: 2010925562

All rights reserved. No part of this work may be reproduced or used in any forms or by any means – graphic, electronic or mechanical, including photocopying or information storage and retrieval systems – without written permission from the copyright holder.

Printed in China.
ISBN: 978-0-7643-3232-6

We are interested in hearing from authors with book ideas on related topics.

Published by Schiffer Publishing Ltd.
4880 Lower Valley Road
Atglen, PA 19310
Phone: (610) 593-1777
FAX: (610) 593-2002
E-mail: Info@schifferbooks.com.
Visit our web site at: www.schifferbooks.com
Please write for a free catalog.
This book may be purchased from the publisher.
Please include $5.00 postage.
Try your bookstore first.

In Europe, Schiffer books are distributed by:
Bushwood Books
6 Marksbury Avenue
Kew Gardens
Surrey TW9 4JF
England
Phone: 44 (0) 20 8392-8585
FAX: 44 (0) 20 8392-9876
E-mail: Info@bushwoodbooks.co.uk.

Contents

Introduction 4
Chapter 1 – Aircraft Conceptualization XF7U-1 6
    Aerodynamic Influences from Carrier Design 6
    Aerodynamic Conscripts 14
    Naval Turbojet Development, Westinghouse Overview 16
Chapter 2 – XF7U-1, F7U-1 Development and Description 18
Chapter 3 – Aircraft Structural Design XF7U-1, F7U-1 28
Aircraft Structural General (See Component Breakdown) 31
    Alighting Gear 33
    Body Group 35
    Wing Group 40
    Tail Group 45
    Engine Group 47
Chapter 4 – J34WE-30 Power Equations and Design 48
Chapter 5 – Flight Test XF7U-1, F7U-1 63
    Initial Patuxent River Evaluations 63
    First Modifications 64
    More Testing 65
    Carrier Suitability Tests 66
    Conclusions 69
    Recommendations 73
Chapter 6 – Further Developments of the Cutlass 78
    F7U-2 78
    F7U-3 80
    The Master Plan, Blue Book 83
        AA Priority 87
        A Priority 87
        B Priority 90
        C Priority 94
    Ailavator Control and Feel System 95
    J46-WE-8 A 98
Chapter 7 – F7U-3, 3M Flight Test 106
    Patuxent River Testing 109
    Carrier Suitability Tests 114
    Results 116
    Conclusions 116
    Recommendations 119
    Flight Characteristics 119
Chapter 8 – Cutlass Versatility 124
    F7U-3 M Missile Carrier 125
    Buddy Aerial Refueling System 140
    A2 U-1 150
    V-396 152
Chapter 9 – Stall Spin Testing and Accidents 154
    Stall and Spin Testing 154
    Accidents 158
    Conclusions and Pilot Recollections 163
Chapter 10 – F7U-3 Restoration at the Museum of Flight 164
    Flight Restoration of F7U-3 164
Appendix 1: Specs and Drawings 183

Introduction

The Chance Vought F7U Cutlass celebrated a radical departure from conventional aeronautical design philosophies embraced during the time of its development. Reasons cited for its tailless configuration resulted directly from a phenomenon known as compressibility. This event experienced by some World War II pilots culminated during the advent of a power dive on one's aircraft in excess of 500 knots, or .75 mach. The downwash from high-speed airflow over the wing impacts the horizontal stabilizer and initiates the nose of the aircraft to tuck under (pitch under). This condition produced an inordinately high stick force, too high for the pilot to handle, rendering all control inputs useless. This condition often resulted in disaster for both plane and pilot alike. Since the Cutlass would be operating in the realm of .9 mach it would, therefore, be prudent on behalf of the engineers at Vought to address this problem in a pragmatic manner. The final solution would rest in the complete elimination of the horizontal stabilizer, producing the flying wing design that would ultimately become the aircraft's most distinguishable feature.

Spawned from a day fighter competition elicited on behalf of the U.S. Navy Bureau of Aeronautics (BuAer), six different aircraft companies in all met the 15 April 1946 deadline. The Navy soon awarded Vought the contract on 27 June 1946 for its V-346A tailless design. The first prototype, completed on 10 December 1947, bore the designation XF7U-1 (U for Vought) and was aptly named Cutlass.

Three prototypes were produced, all eventually succumbing to disaster, but not without first revealing some important and relevant data responsible for the development of an improved version, the F7U-3 Cutlass.

With the cancellation of the F7U-1 and stillborn F7U-2, the Dash 3 afforded an overall quantum leap in design over its predecessors and brought further distinction to its unique design by being the host of the following:

First U.S. jet fighter initially designed for the use of afterburners.
First Navy swept-wing jet, and the first to fly in turn from a carrier deck.
First near-sonic Navy fighter.
First tailless aircraft to be mass produced for U.S. service use.
First Navy fighter to utilize an irreversible power control system, or elevator and aileron (alleviator).
First U.S. jet aircraft to achieve super-sonic separation of stores.
First Naval fighter with a steerable nose wheel.
First U.S. jet fighter to carry rockets in an under fuselage pack.

The Cutlass program existed in a point in time where Vought designers routinely thought out of the box and were not afraid to experiment with new and often divergent design concepts. Regardless of rumors that the Cutlass was heavily influenced by an influx of German aerodynamic research by the Arado Company during its development, it can be credited to an all American effort devoid of any outside influence. The Cutlass, one such example of this effort, significantly contributed to the aerodynamic gene pool existing during this exciting, though turbulent, time in aircraft design history.

Chapter 1

Aircraft Conceptualization XF7U-1

The design and development of the F7U Cutlass celebrated a radical departure from conventionally accepted design practices embraced at this juncture in aeronautical history. Its design directly resulted from the novel, resourceful, and exceptional engineering skills possessed by Vought engineers in the resolution of an aerodynamic event known as compressibility.

The Cutlass began life when the U.S. Navy endeavored to obtain a day fighter, jet propelled, and higher in overall performance than existing production fighters currently in use. Therefore, on behalf of BuAer a day fighter competition initiated and elicited a response from six different aircraft companies. Twelve different designs met the 15 April 1946 deadline. Eventually Vought designs culminated in the V-346A, B, and C and were selected over the Douglas 565 entry.

Aerodynamic Influences from Carrier Design
One must bear in mind the divergent design philosophies employed at this point in time by the United States Air Force and Navy. In retrospect, the Air Force mind set resided in intercontinental range bombers, fighter-bombers, and short-range interceptors, affording generous amounts of runway lengths translating in to numerous support facilities and bases. Conversely, the Navy operated its share of naval air stations supporting the likes of its specially designed aircraft, the bulk of which were operated from the heaving decks of aircraft carriers. Jet propelled aircraft were at this time in their infancy, and often required extra care and pampering just to operate. Serious doubt existed as to whether jet propelled aircraft could, in fact, operate adequately in the cramped, often constrained shipboard environment experienced during lengthy deployments. Naval aircraft architects confronted the issues of limited runway deck length, and the size and space limitations imposed on them by the aircraft carriers' overall design, in pragmatic and novel ways.

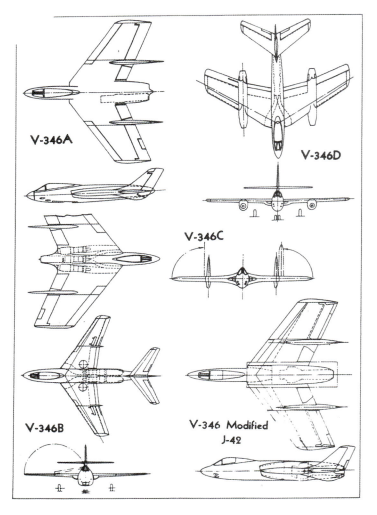

The conceptualization phase, to some, is most important and creative in the vetting of this design process. Each proposal is uniquely varied in scope as well as concept. *Courtesy Author*

The result and final decision based upon the V 346A proposal is evident in this photo of the first XF7U-1, prototype BuNo 122472. *Courtesy Author*

One such example of this resourcefulness found relevance in the early design configurations of the Cutlass. Vought's winning entry, culminating in the V-346A, B, and C (V-346A eventually selected), reflected this type of thinking, producing the XF7U-1.

The V-346A design consisted of a twin-engine tailless posture weighing a robust 14,300 pounds, sporting 6,500 feet per minute rate of climb and employing a top speed of 620 knots. Twin vertical stabilizers, one on each wing, provided the longitudinal stability needed for flight.

The V-346B utilized a conventional configuration employing a traditional tail in concert with two Westinghouse J34 turbojets. Weight estimates dwelled around 15,700 pounds, with a rate of climb of 5,800 feet per minute and a top speed of 605 knots.

The V-345C is tailless in overall design architecture, similar to the V-346A, except it enshrouded three J34 engines, one located along each wing root attachment and augmented by the third centerline located engine.

The V-346D—yes, there existed a modified conventionally designed aircraft that did not make the final selection. It incorporated the use of three J34s: one located under each wing in nacelles, culminating in the third J34 positioned securely in the fuselage. It weighed a hefty 20,950 pounds, possessing a rate of climb of 7,000 feet per second and a top speed of 610 knots.

The V-346 modified—this design drew some consideration and retained a tailless configuration consistent to that of the V-346A entry and powered by a solitary Pratt & Whitney J42 centrifugal flow turbojet.

XF7U-1 No. 122472 shown in a high speed turn sports twin wing tip instrumentation booms, which in turn become a source of concern early on in its flight test program. *Courtesy Vought Heritage Foundation*

The USS *Langley* (CV-1), America's first functioning aircraft carrier, flew its share of Grumman biplane fighters from her 542 foot long deck, circa 1929. *Courtesy The National Naval Aviation Museum*

One of the more pressing issues faced by Vought engineers dealt with the limited runway space afforded to by Naval architects at that time. Back in the late 1920s and early '30s, the USS *Langley* (CV-1) flew Grumman biplane fighters from her 542-foot long flight deck, where takeoff distance did not pose an appreciable problem. Hence came World War II, and the role of Naval fighters changed—and so did their weight. No matter how well a fighter is designed, it is in a constant state of evolution, thus inviting heavier airframes in this process. By virtue, this additional weight required longer takeoff distances not readily available from existing aircraft carriers at that time.

The advent of the hydraulic catapult changed matters in this regard. A high pressure hydraulic cylinder attached by cable to the aircraft and imparted the added energy for that aircraft to obtain flight. Since design work began in late 1945, the Cutlass would initially have to operate from the World War II Essex class carriers incorporating this method of operation. Sweeping the wings to 35° required higher takeoff speed, thus necessitating the need for hydraulic catapults. The type of hydraulic catapult used was designated H4B. Introduced by the British, steam powered catapults, augmented by angled flight decks, eventually replaced their hydraulic counterparts, thus establishing themselves as permanent fixtures in the inventory of modern aircraft carrier design.

Jet-propelled Naval aircraft were heavier than their piston powered propeller driven brethren. Jet aircraft carried twice the fuel of propeller driven aircraft with only 60 to 70 percent of their endurance. The use of swept wings on a Naval jet propelled, high performance fighter, unheard of at the time, posed unique challenges, one of which would be landing and recovery of the craft.

The USS *Lexington* (CV-16), an Essex class carrier circa 1942, represents initially how constrained the operational environment would be for the Cutlass, thus significantly influencing its overall design architecture. *Courtesy The National Naval Aviation Museum*

The USS *Lexington* (CV-16) represented home, with a new post WWII angled flight deck sporting steam catapults and its complement of jet fighters. *Courtesy The National Naval Aviation Museum*

Right side view of this promising contender reveals the side of the leading edge slats, which provided much needed low speed handling, especially at high angles of attack. *Courtesy Vought Heritage Foundation*

As previously discussed, the Cutlass maintained its overall tailless configuration in order to deal with compressibility issues plaguing high-speed aircraft designers at that time. The Cutlass didn't possess a set of landing flaps, which are critical for retaining low speed stability and control, especially during landing and approaches to a heaving carrier deck. Extremely limited runway space, synonymous with the Essex class of carriers, and the influx of higher V_{PA} (approach speeds) initiated the introduction of high lift devices. One such device, called the Leading Edge Slat,

The elongated nose gear oleo strut is quite apparent through inspection, and necessitated a higher angle of attack needed for lift, especially off the short end of a carrier deck. *Courtesy of Author*

resided along the leading edge of the wing (the entire wing in the case of the Cutlass). When fully extended it allowed the redirection of the ensuing airflow over the entire wing. This afforded better boundary layer control flow, offsetting the onset of a stall. The Cutlass also sported a rather elongated nose gear landing strut that enhanced this vehicle's angle of attack, enabling the Cutlass to operate at its best lift to drag ratio and greatly increasing overall lateral and longitudinal control during landing and takeoff.

The Vought F4U Corsair, "The Sweet Heart of Okinawa," represented the zenith of piston powered fighter technology. Eventually deemed unfit for carrier use due to the torque from its massive 13 foot Hamilton standard propeller, it found its prowess from land bases in the pacific during WWII. *Courtesy The National Naval Aviation Museum*

The Grumman F8F Hellcat, predecessor to the F4F Wildcat, capitalized on the weakness of the Japanese zero. Sporting an 18 cylinder Pratt & Whitney R-2800 piston powered radial engine, it experienced superior performance to that of its wildcat brethren. This was achieved through extended speed and overall maneuvering ability. *Courtesy The National Naval Aviation Museum*

World War II produced carrier based aircraft, the likes of which include the hellcat, Corsair, and Bearcat fighters, as well as the Helldiver and TBF Avenger. These straight winged aircraft landed on carrier decks utilizing the "flat-paddled" approach, which in turn was controlled by a landing signal officer (LSO). The purpose of the LSO was to indicate to the pilot of the approaching aircraft whether the aircraft was too high, or low, to the left or right, or if it was too fast or slow.

The Grumman F8F Bear Cat essentially marked the end of the piston powered fighters for the Army Air Corps and Navy, and was introduced rather late in WWII; it would later find its nich in air racing. This lightweight fighter also incorporated the use of the Pratt & Whitney R-2800 radial engine, which vastly improved its power to weight ratio. *Courtesy The National Naval Aviation Museum*

Aircraft approach signals were conveyed to the pilot through certain positional cueing of the paddles initiated by a landing signal officer (LSO). Through this positional cueing the pilot could ascertain if his craft was too high or low, and too fast or slow. *Courtesy The National Naval Aviation Museum*

The approach signals were conveyed by certain positional cueing of the paddles initiated by the LSO. The Cutlass would no doubt operate in this same operational environment.

In 1953, eight years after design work began on the Cutlass, McDonnell Aircraft Corporation indulged in a limited approach speed study. The study aircraft, their XF-88A Voodoo (precursor to the F-101), performed a carefully controlled series of tests to determine the minimum V_{PA} and aptly applied it to carrier jet aircraft as well. This is the result of such tests:

A. The flight path correction altitude that pilots found desirable resided at a minimum approach speed to be 50 foot.
B. Corrections to this flight path should only be limited by stall.
C. The 50-foot altitude gain depends on approximately 43% of the load factor regardless of the rapidity of longitudinal input use.
D. The maximum angle of attack (AoA) or lift coefficient obtained during the 50-foot altitude gain (flight path correction) is equivalent to the AoA for the level of flight attained from the 50-foot gain in altitude. Mathematically speaking, the following equations sum up the study.

In mathematical form:

$W_1 = W_2 = W$ where W = aircraft weight
$P_1 = P_2 = P$ where P = air density
$S_1 = S_2 = S$ where S = wing area
$W/0.5\ PS = C_{L1}V_1^2 = C_{L2}V_2^2$ where C_L = lift coefficient where V^2 = square of aircraft speed

In the pull up maneuver C_L is increasing (angle of attack), and velocity—or aircraft speed—is decreasing due to drag, when combining these factors. The speed during this 50-foot flare maneuver V_2 can be determined:

$V_2 = \sqrt{V_1^2\ C_{L1} / C_{L2}}$

The F7U-3 and 3M were the only variant of the Cutlass to mature to squadron use. The landing performance of the Dash 3 Cutlass would evolve into the following data:

V_S/V_{PA} = 105 @ 23/117 @ 21 K

In their infancy, Navy jets suffered unmercifully due to their underpowered and slow responding turbojets. One accepted maneuver during approach called the backside, or use of the throttle engaging the after burners, provided the extra power during landing approach. If for some reason the pilot was waved off, or could not land, he would have sufficient power to re-emerge in the landing pattern and try again.

Three regions exist in regard to power setting as air speed bleeds off. From the front side the pilot doesn't require much power to facilitate changes in AoA. This part of the entire maneuver is the easiest. As more air speed diminished in the bucket region, variations in throttle (or longitudinal stick) would effect inordinately large and unacceptable changes in air speed. Pilots experiencing this region found it more objectionable than any other part of the thrust curve. As the indicated air speed approached the aircraft stall speed the backside use of the throttle was imperative and difficult to execute with significant precision.

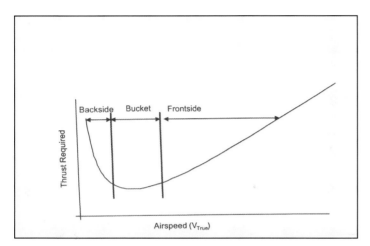

This thrust required airspeed chart conveys how a jet pilot managed the overall energy of his craft through the skillful manipulation of the engine throttles, especially during a carrier approach and landing. *Courtesy Author*

Cutlass pilots vigorously applied these techniques, especially the backside approach, which was the most popular in lieu of the aircraft's underpowered Westinghouse J46 WE-8 turbojets.

Aerodynamic Conscripts
The design of the Cutlass called for a .9+ mach maximum flight envelope. Sonic and transonic aircraft designs considered at this juncture in aviation history featured either short, stubby, tapered or swept wings depending on available data. Contrary to popular belief, the Cutlass did not use captured German aeronautical data from the Arado Company. Dr. Schoolfield, Chief Aerodynamicist for Vought, stipulated "it was an entirely home grown effort devoid of any outside influences." When German aeronautical data became available Vought engineers did examine all relevant documents. It did not, though, influence the design outcome of the Cutlass in any manner. One design feature became apparent; swept wings were going to be employed in its overall design in order to increase the aircraft's critical mach number.

The critical mach number, quite simply, is the mach number of the aircraft in flight at which the local mach number becomes 1.0 over some point of the wing. When an aircraft exceeds this value shock waves form over the wing and large changes in the aerodynamic moments and forces occur. High amounts of drag propagate from the airframe, thus requiring more power to overcome.

Sweeping the wing increased the aircraft's critical mach number, thereby reducing the onset of adverse aerodynamic effects. The use of wing sweep first suggested by Dr. Busemann in 1935 laid the groundwork for future research in swept wing design.

The effects of sweeping the wing on the critical mach number of finite wings involved the aspect ratio (wingspan/average wing chord) and airfoil thickness. When a swept angle is applied, a simple cosine relationship is employed somewhat overestimating the effects of sweep angle on the critical mach number.

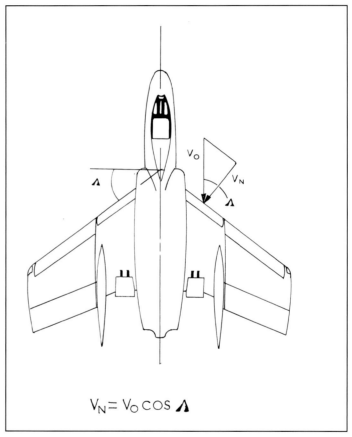

$V_N = V_O \cos \Lambda$ determines the aircraft's critical mach number, especially through its leading edge sweep angle. The critical mach number helps the designer achieve a better understanding of his vehicle's true aerodynamic potential. *Courtesy Author*

By sweeping the wing of the Cutlass and eliminating the horizontal stabilizer altogether, Vought engineers could manage the high speed shock waves produced in more effective ways, yielding a thicker wing and lower aspect ratio. Wing area remained respective throughout this trade off process. Employing the use of a constant chord, low aspect ratio wing in concert with a rudimentary automatic control system (later introduced) in conjunction with Leading Edge Slats helped control the span-wise movement of air propagated by a stall occurring at large angles of attack and at low approach speeds.

Wing flow model and supporting test apparatus is mounted on the upper side of a P 51 wing. A directional vane is mounted to facilitate cleaner air flow to the test article. *Courtesy Author*

In 1945 the availability of transonic wind tunnels were in short supply. So how did the Cutlass program achieve and maintain its aggressive design posture without the use of such devices? The answer lies with Dr. Robert R. Gilruth, who is the father of the "Free Fall Method" and the "Wing Flow Method." The latter, vigorously pursued by Vought, attained real time and useful data towards the design of the Cutlass.

The wing-flow method involved a small model mounted on the upper surface of the wing of a fighter aircraft. The pilot would initiate a dive from high altitudes, pulling out at a high, but safe, mach number, rendering a flow over that region of the wing to transonic and supersonic speed. This method found great popularity in its use because a region of reasonably uniform flow existed over the wing in the area of the test model.

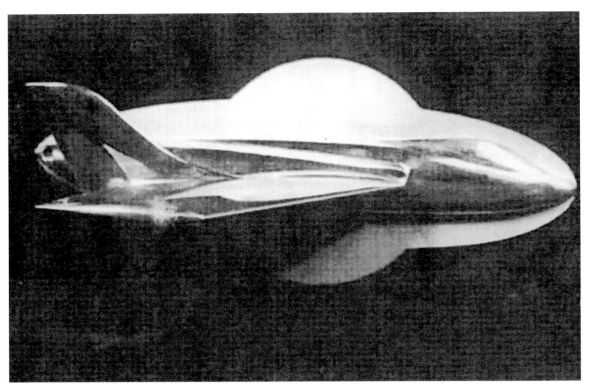

This is a wing flow model of the Vought F7U-1 Cutlass. A half model is used and securely fastened to glove contour the curvature of the P-51 wing. Testing provided accurate results in real time, as opposed to conventional wind tunnel testing. *Courtesy Author*

In the case of the F7U model, a special glove was built to the contour of the wing of a P-51 Mustang. The mounting of a "half model" of the Cutlass was armed with and attached to a vacuum-operated automobile windshield wiper motor, whose sole function was to oscillate the model at one cycle per second. This covered an entire range of angle of attack and mach number in a single 30-second dive. Balances and other measuring equipment were used in their tests as well. This singular event provided more data than a month of conventional wind tunnel testing. Criticism did exist from some wind tunnel specialists, citing the small size of the model and lack of definable boundaries to surround the flow. What did transpire from the "wing flow" technique resulted in data, continuous through a range of variables. Consequently, small irregularities or nonlinear ties in the aerodynamic forces could in fact be calculated with as much accuracy as needed. This didn't exist in conventional wind tunnel technology at the time. The "wing flow" technique also allowed detailed studies in the affects of rate of change of variables as well as that of steady valves. When studying actual flight, the involvement of real time change conditions were measured by the "wing flow" technique, not so for wind tunnels.

Naval Turbojet Development, Westinghouse Overview
U.S. Naval turbojet genesis began with Westinghouse Corporation's once mighty Aviation Gas Turbine Division. This company achieved many firsts, essentially laying the groundwork and displaying America's technical bravado in turbojet design, especially during World War II, where the historical focus remained predominately with Germany and England. Quite frankly, the Westinghouse Corporation built America's first axial flow turbojet without any technical assistance or influence from England or Germany. As history would provide, the Westinghouse Corporation's involvement in gas turbine design began with the Durand Special Committee on jet propulsion and was encouraged by a Navy letter of intent. Westinghouse interest was further enhanced by the promising research from Westinghouse engineer Winston R. New on gas turbine design. Armed with this influx of new data, Dr. Stewart Way prepared a proposal to the Durand Special Committee outlining the development of a gas turbine, greatly influencing the decision on behalf of Westinghouse in committing to developing this new technology. As time allowed, Westinghouse participation in the Durand Special Committee on jet propulsion subsequently indicated further interest in conducting future research. Westinghouse's Manager of Development Engineering, Reinout P. Kroon, contacted F. T. Hague, Manager of Engineering, and formulated a specific plan of approach involving the Navy occurring on 13 October 1941. On 8 December 1941, Westinghouse representatives visited the Navy Bureau of Aeronautics in the quest of further assisting the Navy's engine development program. The Navy responded on 7 January 1942 with a letter of intent outlining a proposal, "The Study and Design" of a small booster turbojet to assist carrier aircraft on short takeoffs. Westinghouse was authorized on 2 October 1942 to construct two 19-inch diameter axial flow

turbojet engines designed for this specific purpose.

Subsequently, Mr. Kroon and his staff's efforts culminated in the design of Westinghouse's first engine, the 19A, dubbed "The Yankee." First tested on 19 March 1943, the Yankee quickly evolved into the 19B, with eventual designs bearing fruit in three distinct sizes: 9.5 inches, 19 inches, and 24 inches in diameter respectively. The 9.5A and B were slated for missiles and aircraft, bearing the Naval designation J32. The 19B eventually became the J30 and possessed a 10-stage compressor, and was rated at 1,600 lb. Tested under a Martin Marauder, it eventually powered the McDonnell FH-1 Phantom.

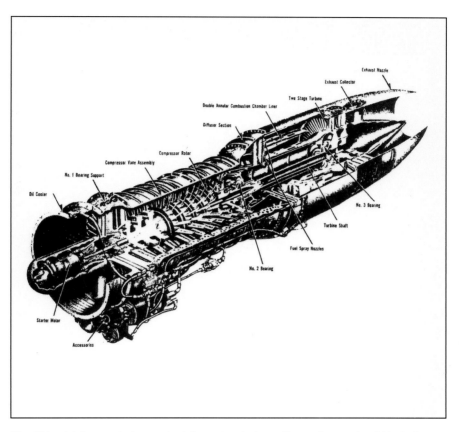

The J34 axial flow turbojet resulted from the tireless efforts of some key Westinghouse engineering personnel. They, in fact, displayed America's technical bravado in a time where world attention focused on England and Germany. *Courtesy Author*

The J34 would power the Cutlass in its early version, predicating the XF7U-1 and F7U-1 designs respectfully. It became apparent that aeronautical development had begun to eclipse the power brokers of turbojet design. Airframe weight, as well as performance, clearly outpaced turbojet development. This sad but true occurrence gave many procurement officers, as well as defense contractors, a bad bone of contention to gnaw on. Westinghouse would evolve to be the preeminent supplier of turbojets to the United States Navy, only to fall from grace, succumbing to an inability to meet schedules and deliver quality products, and ultimately went out of business.

Chapter 2

XF7U-1 Development and Description

The XF7U-1 Cutlass is best described through the eyes of the U.S. Navy as "an experimental tailless fighter designed for carrier operations and equipped with two Westinghouse 24C (J34) turbojets."

Other more visual features of both the XF7U-1 and F7U-1 would include a swept wing (35° leading edge) of low aspect ratio, and being tailless in overall configuration. Twin vertical stabilizers mounted on the outboard edges of the wing's center section achieved lateral stability. Longitudinal and lateral control was maintained through plain flap-type control surfaces better known as ailevators. Folding wings were a must to facilitate operation and storage above and below the carrier deck. The Cutlass also incorporated the first full hydraulically boosted fight controls

XF7U-1 BU-No 122472 is shown in early flight sporting its twin wing tip instrumentation booms. These were immediately replaced due to severe vibrations encountered on subsequent flights. *Courtesy Author*

featuring a 3000-psi totally irreversible system. It would also support a fully automated flight control system, thus affording additional stability to that aircraft. Located along the leading edge of the wing were fully functional slats which, when employed, provided the low-speed handling qualities needed for landing and takeoff. Slats also, when extended, increases the wind chord, thus enhancing aerodynamic qualities of the wing, especially at low air speeds. The lack of landing flaps only served to employ the use of speed brakes. Two clamshell type speed brakes were located on the trailing edge of each wing—each side of and one between the fuselage and vertical stabilizers. The other two were positioned toward the forward fuselage under the leading edge of the air intake ducts. Other items of particular interest would include a Vought fully pressurized and air conditioned cockpit, tricycle landing gear with a steerable nose wheel, a fixed gun emplacement consisting of four twenty millimeter cannons, and a company designed ejection seat.

XF7U-1 No. 472 (short for 122472) is shown with a new instrumentation boom located on its nose. This replaced the troublesome twin unit previously in use. By virtue of this photo, it would suggest the high performance nature of this aircraft deomstrating its cutting edge technology. *Courtesy Chance Vought Aircraft*

With speed brakes fully deployed this F7U-1 example clearly demonstrates its uniqueness of design and how aesthetically pleasing as well as aerodynamically clean it is in overall appearance. *Courtesy Author*

F7U-1 No. 422, seen here in this three quarter AFT view, clearly outlined the functionality of the speed brake. Also viewed is its uniquely deployed arresting gear. *Courtesy Author*

Aft view of the same aircraft clearly differentiates the clam shell functional effect of these air brakes. The two other speed brakes forward of the intakes were deemed of no practical use and were eventually deleted. *Courtesy Author*

The underside of the wing under each vertical stabilizer housed the main landing gear wheel wells. The nose gear oleo strut, longer in overall length, gave the Cutlass its 9° angle of incidence, further enhancing its high lift capabilities.

Development

As previously stated, the XF7U-1 became a reality from the outgrowth from Vought's advanced engineering work on design V-346. The insistence from Buaer's letter C-00853, dated and submitted to Vought on 25 January 1946, encouraged the airframe manufacturer to submit a proposal for a high performance CF airplane. This letter would include the submission of: "design studies and informal estimates of cost and first flight dates for the design and construction of two or, alternately, three experimental fighter airplanes, plus one article for static tests." Other general requirements involved the following:

Gross weight: That used to obtain the specified radius of action.
Performance (at flight design gross weight):
Maximum speed in level flight (mph) - 650
High speed at military rated thrust (mph) - 600
Maximum rate of climb fpm (feet per minute) - 10,000
Rate of climb at military rated thrust (fpm) - 8,000
Takeoff rate of climb, at sea level and at 95°F, fully loaded
    in landing configuration, flaps and landing gear
    down (fpm) – 500
Wave off rate of climb at sea level, 95°F, fully loaded and
    at an approach speed of 100 mpg (fpm) – 500
Takeoff stalling speed (mph) – 105
Stalling speed in landing configuration/with power off a
    quarter of fuel supply left (mph) – 90
Service ceiling in ft – 40,000
Fighter radius: not less than 300 nautical miles.
Cruising radius: Three hours' endurance at 30,000 ft.
Allowable takeoff stalling speeds with the following
    gross weights:
    22,000 lbs – 105 mph
    24,000 lbs – 102.5 mph
    26,000 lbs – 100 mph
    27,500 lbs – 98 mph
    30,000 lbs – 95 mph
Also guarantees are specified as part of the vetting process:
1. Weight empty.
2. Vmax level flight, military power, flight loading condition.
3. R/C maximum at military power, flight loading condition.
Power off R/C at 115 mph, 95°F, landing gear down, flaps down, T.0 setting at T.0 landing condition.

The XF7U-1 and F7U-1 embraced a single elongated oleo strut incorporating a single steerable nose wheel. XF7U-1's forged wheel yoke wasn't fully enclosed as on its F7U-1 brethren. *Courtesy Jay Miller Collection*

This J34 cut-a-way, seen here next to the Douglas X-3 stiletto, is essentially the same power plant used in the early Cutlass. It offered a substantially higher power to weight ratio than its centrifugal counter parts at a significantly reduced cross section.
Courtesy Author

The Navy, in regard to the power plant, further stipulated:

> The contractor's choice of engines is unlimited within those gas turbines, turbo-jets, rockets or ram jets under development or manufactured in the United States. Engine ratings shall be those approved by the Bureau of Aeronautics. The contractor shall coordinate with the Bureau of Aeronautics the engine installation, performance and weight characteristics he proposed to use prior to proceeding with airplane performance calculations. The Bureau of Aeronautics reserves the right to reject any proposal based on use of a power plant of which there is inadequate evidence to indicate availability in time for the estimate flight date.

The following Table is furnished from Buaer to the controller:

Table 2-1 Table of Available Power Plants

Model	Thrust	Weight	Length	Dia
TG 180	4000lbs	2346lbs	14'10"	39"
I 40	4000lbs	1853lbs	8'7"	48"
24 C*	3000lbs	1185lbs	9'11"	24"

Closing dates for engineering proposals and cost estimates to BuAer were set for 15 April 1946 and 1 May 1946, 12:00 PM respectively. As previously mentioned, Vought submitted four separate proposals culminating in the V-346A, B, C, and D designs. Information obtained from Mr. J. B. Bacsik and Mr. John J. Hospers, then Sales Manager at Vought, confirmed the Navy's choice—that of the V-346A tailless entry. It single-handedly outpaced the Douglas 565 proposal and would set a precedent in design relevance.

It is evident that the Navy was rather smitten with Vought's V-346A design through Mr. Hosper's contact with Admiral L. B. Richardson, Assistant Chief, BuAer, in correspondence sent to Vought's General Manager, Rex Beisel, on 12 April 1946. He "discussed the day fighter proposal V-346 with the Admiral and he was happy to learn that we (Vought) would be in a position to present some interesting and comprehensive designs. I (Mr. Hospers) mentioned tailless aircraft to him and he was interested and appeared to favor the idea."

Subsequently, on 12 April 1946 letter E-1414, over the signature from General Manager Rex B. Beisel, authorized the transmission of the company's informal proposal covering designs V-346A thru D, complete with drawings and a proposal booklet disclosing all descriptive matter. As for the V-346A, which was heavily favored and eventually selected, certain guaranteed specifications were sent forth in lieu of this generalization relating to the tailless concept:

> Studies of the use of the tailless configuration for a high speed fighter, as discussed in enclosure (F), show that appreciable gains in performance and revolution in size may be obtained by this type. It is appreciated that the tailless airplane presents new problems; however, the necessary fundamental characteristics are known and can be attained by careful design. The problems associated with obtaining satisfactory stability and control characteristics should be comparable to those for conventional aircraft incorporating sweepback. The tailless airplane arrangements offer higher performance combined with smaller size and weight than the conventional type with comparable power but they are unconventional.

XF7U-1 No. 474, the third and last of the initial prototypes, is displayed here with open cockpit and nose boom awaiting test flight. The early Cutlass embraced a bat-like thoroughbred appearance and was unlike any design of its contemporaries. *Courtesy Author*

XF7U-1 No. 474 again, further demonstrating its unique aerodynamic design and especially accentuating its twin vertical stabilizers. *Courtesy Author*

Paragraph three simply states the general descriptive nature of the aircraft, supplemented by further comments regarding power plant use. The reasons cited for the selection of the Westinghouse Model 24C find relevance in the following statement. "This unit has lower specific weight and lower specific volume than other available turbojets, and is more adaptable to installation in body and wing section necessary for high critical speeds. Combat power is obtained by producing additional main engine thrust with an afterburning installation mounted in a tailpipe extension of the turbo-jet unit."

Performance guarantees were submitted and were subject to the expressed qualifications that "any design change increasing the weight of the airplane will have an adverse effect on one or more of the guaranteed items of performance."

The introduction of paragraph eight states that ". . . V-346A is considered by the contractor to be the smallest and lightest airplane design capable of meeting the performance requirements (stipulated on the request). This airplane has a takeoff weight of 16,796 pounds and has *significant margins on all performance requirements* of the type specification *except* that it just meets the military rate of climb."

From this proposal, enclosure (E) outlines the following weight and performance guarantees for the V-346A design:

Weight empty as defined in Paragraph 105A
1. Maximum speed in level flight, military combat loading condition, mph – 620.

2. Maximum rate of climb, military thrust, combat loading condition, ft/min – 6,520.
3. Stalling speed without power at sea level, landing loading condition, mph – 89.3.
4. Rate of climb at take-off at 115 mph, 95°F, day, sea level, military thrust, takeoff loading condition, ft/min – 830.

From the Vought Engineering Department Annual Report for 1946, the following information was cited. "In April of this year engineering proposal for the V-346A, B, C and D submitted to the Navy, and on 25 June, 1946, a letter of intent was received for our XF7U-1 airplane. It exists with a low aspect ratio, swept wing (tailless) in configuration powered by two Westinghouse 24C-4B jet units with after burners for combat power." Also noted, "a very successful Navy Mockup Board Meeting was held at Chance Vought from 15 October to 18 October with 37 Navy representatives attending." More information cited from Chapter 4 would include, "an intensive weight control program is being conducted in an effort to keep the airplane at the proposal weight. Preliminary wind tunnel tests have been conducted at M.I.T. and at the David Taylor Model Basin in Washington, and the results have permitted the freezing of the aerodynamic configuration of this airplane."

The publication of NAVAER SD-430, dated 8 July 1946, outlined the detailed specifications in regard to the Model XF7U-1 airplane under Contract No. A(S)-8337. Other more specific details of this contract can be placed in contrast to Vought's original proposal, Letter E-1414. For example, the engines that were specified were Westinghouse J34 WE-22 with rates (military) of 3000 lb static thrust at 12,500 rpm and at sea level.

The "design maximum level of flight speed at sea level" dwelled at 520 knots (or about 600 mph), service ceiling 40,600 ft.

Other milestones involving the development of the XF7-U1 include:

2 October 1945 Preliminary design started.
25 January 1945 Proposal request received from Buaer.
15 April 1946 Engineering proposal submitted.
28 June 1946 Letter of intent received (Contract No. a(s)-8337) for design and construction of the three model XF7U-1.
15 October 1946 Mock-up Board Review.
1 November 1946 Planning and tooling started.
1 December 1946 Design frozen.
15 January 1947 First drawing.
22 February 1947 Fabrication started.
5 December 1947 Engineering completed: Design released (scheduled 10 October 1947).
31 May 1948 Tooling completed.
12 July 1948 #1 airplane shop completed.
29 September 1948 Initial flight #1 (scheduled for July).
Airplane No. 2 XF7U-1 authorized in the original letter of intent, and shop completed on 28 January 1949. Made its first flight on 14 February 1949.

This hangar view reveals the finely sculpted lines of this unidentified Cutlass. More than likely this is the first of 14 of the newly procured F7U-1 Cutlasses that were developed strictly for experimental use. *Courtesy Author*

With the shop completion of XF7U-1 Airplane No. 1, a letter of intent received on 28 July 1948 by Vought from the Navy outlined the provision for 19 more airframes designated F7U-1. Accompanying this directive were explicit design changes spawned from operational deficiencies discovered during the testing of the XF7U-1 aircraft.

Copious amounts of changes highlighted in the contractor's directive vastly effected the overall weight of the new airframe. Included in Supplement No. 1 to SD-430-1 are the following "changes" and are disclosed as follows:

Table 2-2

Topic	Fighter (Combat Fuel)	Fighter (Normal Fuel)
Gross Weight (Not Guaranteed)	18,195lbs	20,523lbs
Fuel Capacity	585 Gal	971 Gal
High Speed In Level Flight At Altitude For Max Speed		
(Military Trust)	549 Knots (631 mph)	
For Normal Thrust	530 Knots (610 mph)	
Stalling Speed @ Sea level Without Power, Gear and Slats Extended	100.5 Knots (116 mph)	
Rate of Climb @ Sea level, Military Thrust (FPM)	5280	
Rate of Climb, Military Thrust, 95°F @ 112 Knots (FPM)	760	
Service Ceiling, Normal Thrust, With Full Load	40,000 Ft	

Almost as quickly as the contract was issued it was amended to only 14 airframes, and would contain the Westinghouse J34 WE32 turbojet.

F7U-1 No 419, shown here in flight, sports a glossy Navy blue exterior accentuated by an all natural metal finish in the afterburner section. Checkered vertical fins further identify this craft, accenting an all white nose finish with a red arrow.
Courtesy Author

This view of 416 clearly displays its constant chord wing while maintaining a notable leading edge sweep. Lateral and longitudinal control is maintained by ailevators functioning both as ailerons and elevators located outboard on the wings.
Courtesy Author

The first of 14 airplanes designated F7U-1, CVA #1, accepted on 23 June 1950 and delivered 8 December 1950, immediately began its flight test program. In turn, the last example, CVA #14, accepted 8 December 1952 and delivered 21 December 1952, was eventually relegated to training squadrons in favor of the more advanced F7U-3. It must be noted that these 14 examples of aircraft designated F7U-1 were considered experimental as well. Hence, the small quantity of aircraft accrued to the differential between deliveries of CV #1 and CV #14 transpires over a 32-month period.

F7U1 Airplane Number 1 (Vought SerNo 10264/ Navy 124415)
The Engineering Status Report on 23 January 1950 indicated the near completion of its CVA #1 airframe. The aircraft existed in sustenance of 15 assembled, 75% complete with 6 sub-assembled, 100% complete. However, in Paragraph 15 of this subsequent report outlined the work remaining. ". . . to be done consists of hydraulic cycle, electrical operation, rigging, installation of pilot's seat, installation of engine, sliding section, pressurization, check out of main fuselage fuel cell, engine access doors and shakedown."

CVA Letter E-775, 16 March 1950 suggests a modification program including five "fixes" (revisions). They include a newly revised surface control system, the installation of a yaw-rate damper increasing the overall fin and rudder area, a redesigned nose gear oleo strut, and the installation of dual wing catapult hooks. More changes were in store for this aircraft. Thirteen changes existed per day between 7 April and 3 May 1950. Engineering memo 402, submitted on 30 March 1950 listed 35 changes alone, thus detailing the magnitude and scope as to the changes taking place to this particular aircraft.

Another view from the top of example 422 shows its basic but functional plan form. *Courtesy Tom Cathcart*

Cutlass No 422, the eighth production example out of a procurement lot of 14 F7U-1 aircraft, differs little in appearance to that of its predecessor, the XF7U-1. Copious amounts of engineering changes did in fact take place, a necessary progression culminating in the F7U-3. *Courtesy Tom Cathcart*

Example 422 flies effortlessly and expresses itself through its finely tailored airframe, establishing its potency as a contender as a future Naval fighter. *Courtesy Jay Miller Collection*

F7U1 Airplane Number 2 (Vought SerNo 10265/ Navy 124416)

Likewise, the aircraft fared none the better than its counterpart in varying percentages of completion. This became obvious from the Engineering Status Report filed on 23 January 1950. Engineering Memo 401, several months later on 30 March 1950, outlined the limited flight testing to be conducted at Ardmore the following day on CVA #2. This memo also allowed for 20 additional equipment installations and modifications to take place after the initial flight.

Engineering Memo EM-448, 11 April 1950, extended by one week the subsequent test time for the expressed interest of investigating other component changes to be incorporated on later Cutlass designs. This would include an enlarged vertical tail and certain yawed flight studies specially targeted for this future use.

F7U1 Airplane Number 2 (Vought SerNo 10266/ Navy 124417)

As a result of an accident suffered on 6 July 1950, seven airframe changes were stipulated and further documented in Engineering memo (EM) 1130, released on 5 October 1950. As a consequence all 14 F7U-1s were finally modified to the same exacting standards as to the first airframe, laying the groundwork for the final production model, the F7U-3. Several F7U-1s made available for carrier trials only served as a test bed, providing much needed information and furthering the design of the Cutlass.

F7U-1 415, the first production aircraft in the initial lot of 14 examples and eventually slated for carrier suitability tests on USS *Midway* (CVB-41) at the hands of LCDR Edward L. Feightner. *Courtesy Author*

This lonely Cutlass is in the company of some well built F4U-5N Corsairs at Hensley field, circa 1950. Chance Vought aircraft has strived to and has developed super fighters for the U.S. Navy. *Courtesy Author*

Chapter 3

Structural Design XF7U-1 F7U-1

The XF7U-1 and F7U-1 were both single seat, carrier-based, high-speed, jet propelled fighters designed from the onset for the U.S. Navy by the Chance Vought Aircraft Company. Both aircraft, in turn, employed stressed skin semi-monocoque construction, accentuating its fully cantilevered mid-positioned wing and twin vertical stabilizers.

Stressed skin semi-monocoque construction, though not new in concept, proved to be the most efficient and proficient method of aircraft assembly, yielding the lightest and strongest airframe available during the Cutlass' developmental period. The origins of stressed skin semi-monocoque construction found credence with a Swiss engineer named Ruchonnet, which in turn curried favor by a Frenchman named Louis Bchereau in the fabrication of the Le monocoque depression monoplane built in 1912. Further exploited in 1916 by the German Albratros Company in the construction of their Model D. Va Biplane, Jack Northrop

Lined up in a sequence progression defined the assembly and production line for each of the subsequent 14 production F7U-1 aircraft. *Courtesy Vought Heritage Center*

seized upon this research, and in 1927 developed the Lockheed Vega. Northrop, true to his reputation as a gifted designer, further developed this concept into aluminum wing and fuselage skins, as well as fuselage bulkheads and wing ribs. This yielded an entire aircraft built exclusively from aluminum. However, it must be noted that this concept of stressed skin structure first found relevance from Adolph Rohrbach's theories on stressed skin wing structures around 1920. Northrop's concept of a riveted aluminum wing and fuselage skins allowed the aircraft's entire structure to react to bending, compression, and tension loads experienced throughout the entire flight envelope.

The prominent fighters residing in U.S. Navy inventories at the end of World War II were the Grumman F6F Hellcat, F8F Bearcat, and Vought's F4U Corsair. All airframes involved could maintain a robust +12g load factor at best and were renown for their ruggedness. The F7U Cutlass also began life at this point in time and, although not held to the same strength standards as its predecessors, it became agonizingly apparent during its first set of carrier trials. The Cutlass, designed for 600-knot+ operation, invokes inherently higher dynamic loading than its piston powered, propeller-driven predecessors. With the involvement of a 35°-wing sweep, the wing thickness ratio of the Cutlass faired lower than that of the Hellcat, Bearcat, or Corsair. Sweeping the wing invited a greater structural span than a straight wing sporting the same area and aspect ratio. Sweeping the wing also initiated additional torsion due to the direction of the applied loads acting significantly aft on the wing root. This would suggest the incorporation of a heavier wing in the natural progression of aircraft design in relation to the entire aircraft weight. This, however, has not been the case. Quite the opposite has occurred. In fact, wing structures have been made lighter. The Cutlass incorporated the advancement in new aircraft building materials and supported the use of higher local working stresses in compression to allow for the advent of higher wing and fuselage skin loadings to occur. When compared to a North American P-51B's wing structural weight to its overall take off weight, the F7U-1, although vastly heavier and larger in size, runs around 1% lighter in wing weight tow. This is in lieu of its staggering increase in wing area, twice as much as that of the Mustang.

Lockheed Vega on display at the Smithsonian Air and Space museum conveys its clean lines and simplicity of design. First to use molded and bonded formed plywood structural skins, they proved rather proficient but often yielded to rot. *Courtesy Smithsonian*

Left side view of the Vega reveals its robust and stout design and demonstrates its roughness, but it still retains its fixed landing gear. *Courtesy Smithsonian*

This Lockheed Sirius circa 1927 shares similar design lines to that of the Vega. Its abrupt stoutness is apparent. *Courtesy Smithsonian*

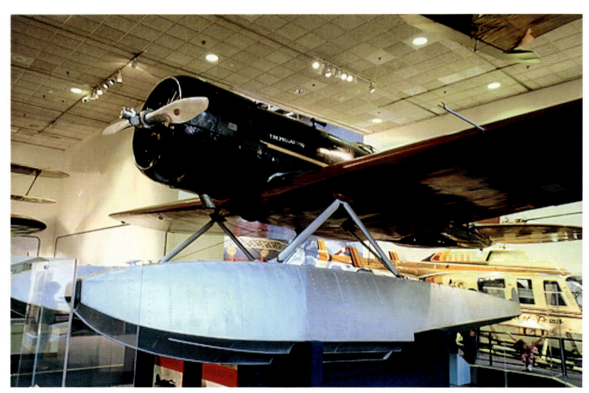

Another view of the Lockheed Sirius again reminds us of its structural stoutness, and it proved to be an efficient and dependable structural design. *Courtesy Smithsonian*

Table 3-1
**Comparsion of Wing Structural Weights of the
North American P-51 B and Vought F7U Cutlass.**

	P-51 B	F7U-1
Take Off Weight (Tow)	8660lbs	22,755lbs
Span	37Ft	38Ft 8 in
Wing Area	236Ft²	496ft²
Quarter Chord Sweep	0°	35°
Wing Root thickness	15%	12%
Wing Weight	1,260lbs	3,136lbs
Wing Weight Tow%	14.5%	13.7%

By the onset of 1946, aircraft structures were intrinsically fabricated essentially by wrapping relatively thin skins over a finely developed internal framework, yielding ease of construction. While the Cutlass designed in this time frame essentially employed the same type of construction methodology, it also embraced new and novel manufacturing techniques. The advent of higher speeds soon to be experienced initiated higher flight loads, inviting the use of thicker structural skins to be utilized in its overall assembly architecture. Once common practice soon yielded to new techniques like pre-forming through rolling, and later by stretched forming. Spot welding the longerons (stringers) to the skins made way for lighter structurally efficient skins than their fully riveted counterparts. This highly specialized process produced a superior surface finish free from any irregularities. By virtue of this technique, the need for rivets and their stress rising holes they produce was eliminated, greatly reducing fatigue in the overall airframe. Integral construction methods are, quite simply, the ability to combine many structural functions in a single complex part to conform within its available airframe location.

Materials

The XF7U-1 and F7U-1 employed generous amounts of aluminum and magnesium alloy in their overall structures. New materials called metalite and fabrilite were developed to further aid in the overall reduction in structural weight. Stainless steel (used in the afterburner section) and acrylic plastic (cockpit) were incorporated as well.

Materials definition: one of the primary structural materials utilized in the airframe of both aircraft is aluminum. Standards set by the Aluminum Company of America (ALCOA) help define the grades of alloy through alloy agents. Like steel, aluminum alloys follow a set standard of composition and manufacture. For example, Z4-S-T-4, written Z4S-T4, states: the number "24" specifies the composition, the letter "S" denotes the metal is wrought (not cast), "T" signifies temper, and the number "4" is a subdivide of temper.

Metalite

Metalite is probably the U.S. aircraft industry's first attempt at a truly composite building material. Existing as a sandwich material consisting of a low-density balsa wood core bonded on to both sides of high strength aluminum faces, it is used primarily for structural skins on the Cutlass. The bonding process exists with the application of special adhesives applied perpendicularly on both sides of the grain of the balsa core to the aluminum alloy faces. Only through the advent of controlled pressures and temperature can metalite truly be realized. The faces used in the fabrication of the metalite structural skins consist exclusively of 75S-T6 aluminum alloy. Additional bonding is achieved through the generous use of phenolic resin and external aluminum alloy. Most metalite panels employ the use of mahogany inserts where fasteners are used.

Magnesium Alloy

Due to the high strength/low weight ratio of magnesium alloy, it found favor with the designers at Vought as the principal structural material used in the fabrication of the Cutlass. Unlike its aluminum alloy counterpart, the strength and hardness of magnesium alloy sheets cannot be improved upon by heat-treating. While most of the formed aluminum alloy parts rely solely upon heat-treating and aging operations, they can, in fact, be hot formed from magnesium alloy in one operation, subsequently without the advent of heat-treating if obtained directly from magnesium alloy.

Fabrilite

Fabrilite, simply, is another composite structural material principally composed of woven glass cloth impregnated with synthetic resins cured under controlled temperatures and pressures. In some instances a low density core such as balsa wood is used. Fabrilite in solid laminate is used in the nose hatch of the F7U-1 aircraft. This material consists of two or more piles of resin impregnated glass fabric (fiberglass) bonding into this solid member. Fabrilites' sandwiched construction can be found on the fin and rudder sections of this aircraft respectively, and consists of a balsa wood core residing between the laminated faces of a fiberglass, to which bonding occurs. Bolted sandwich assemblies include mahogany inserts for rivet and bolt installations. It should be noted that fabrilite assemblies should be handled with care, devoid of any rough treatment when in use.

Corrosion Resistant Steel

Stainless steel, better known as 18-8 stainless steel (18 percent chromium and 8 percent nickel), is best utilized in the aft section of the structure where the turbojet with afterburners are located. Stainless steel is used because of its resistance to inter-granular corrosion due to high temperatures.

Acrylic Sheet Plastic

Acrylic sheet plastic, better known as Plexiglas (AN-P-44), is used in the fabrication of the sliding canopy and the side panels of the windshield in the F7U-1 aircraft. The commercial grade of Plexiglas is also known as Lucite.

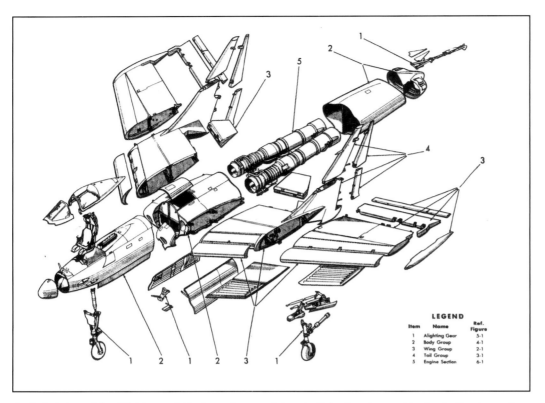

Exploded view of the F7U-1 reveals the legend sequentially prioritizing its subassembles for further inspection. *Courtesy Author*

The XF7U-1 and F7U-1 airframes were identical, except for some slight improvements on the F7U-1 structure. Each model of the aircraft were designed and manufactured in sub-assemblies, and will be further discussed in terms of these assemblies relating specifically to the F7U-1 structural configuration. They are:

1. Alighting gear.
2. Body group.
3. Wing group.
4. Tail group.
5. Engine section.

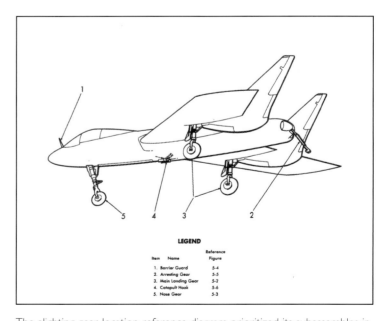

The alighting gear location reference diagram prioritized its subassembles in accordance of functional importance. *Courtesy Author*

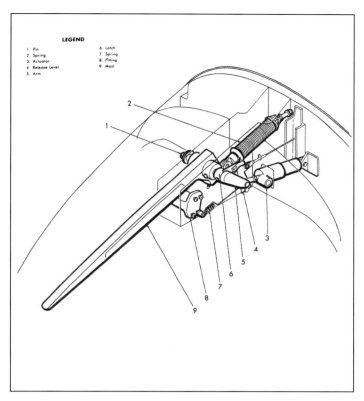

The Barrier Guard's sole purpose is to engage the activated strap of the Davis Barrier in the event of the nose gear failing to deploy or collapsing upon landing. *Courtesy Author*

Alighting Gear

The alighting gear consists of the following components: the barrier group, which is attached to the upper nose section of the fuselage; arresting gear, which is positioned on the extreme aft upper tail section; the main landing gear, diametrically positioned in the wing center section; the catapult hook, located in the lower fuselage approximately at station 210.8; and finally the nose gear, which is located in the bottom of the forward fuselage.

The barrier guard is an aluminum alloy mast, which lies flush in a slot located in the upper side of the nose cone of the aircraft. The guard's sole purpose is to engage the activation strap of the Davis Barrier in the event of the nose gear's failure to deploy or collapse upon landing. When the arresting gear control handle is lowered to the down position a cable releases the barrier guard latch, thus enabling the barrier to spring into a full upright position. When the control handle is placed in the "up" position a small hydraulic cylinder is engaged, therefore lowering the guard to its fully retracted position and further engaging the latch lever, locking it in position.

The arresting gear is the hook, so to speak, that, upon release during a carrier landing, engages the arresting cable on the deck in order to bring the aircraft to a complete, but abbreviated, stop. This gear is comprised of a folding hook, a retraction mechanism, and a support. Because the hook folds, it incorporates a joint which is strategically placed in the upper tail cone at fuselage station 145. This entire assembly embodies a hook point, a tubular steel lower shank that, in turn, is welded to the hook point. This entire assembly is further augmented by the inclusion of an upper shank fabricated from forged steel, a spur gear, and a cam end fitting to support the upper shank (and for activation). An arresting cable release mechanism—a tendon cable and pulley installation—further facilitates the gear's use. Upon activation, the hook is extended by the use of a hydraulic cylinder which actuates a gear rack, rotating the upper shank of the arresting hook mechanism and unfolding it aft and in the downward position. A dashpot is employed on the activating cylinder to absorb and dampen the energy generated by the mass of the aircraft upon landing. When in the non-operational mode the entire assembly is retracted in the upper tail section by three fairings. The first fairing attaches to the lower shank and accelerates it to the extended position. The two remaining fairings are attached to the yoke and pivot upward, initiating the full extension of the arresting gear.

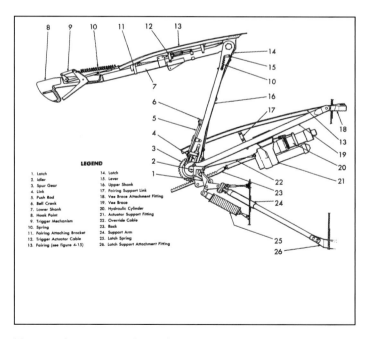

The arresting gear, upon inspection, reveals its inherent complexity and lack of overall strength. After initial carrier trials on F7U-1 arrested landing the mechanism was deemed too fragile for further use. *Courtesy Author*

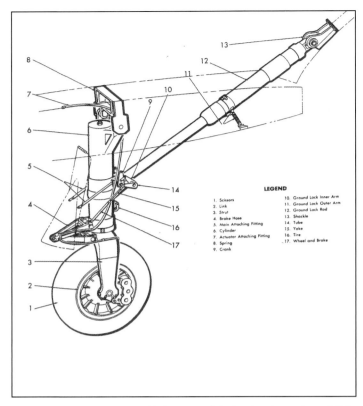

The main landing gear assembly is responsible for the absorption of flight loads upon landing and the aircraft's forward mobility in obtaining flight. *Courtesy Author*

Main Landing Gear

The main landing gear consists of two oleo struts that are actuated hydraulically for the absorption of aircraft loads upon landing. Accompanying these struts are two wheels, each sporting an 8-ply, non-skid, 30 x 7.7 inch tire and brake that fully retracts into the lower fin stub. There are two fin stubs per aircraft. The main landing gear wheel well doors are clamshell in nature and involve the use of two doors per well. Of particular note, the doors, upon landing, open for the exiting gear to lock into position, only to be closed to further relieve drag during this operation. There is a portion of landing gear assembly that houses the forward fairing and remains locked on the struts in both extended or retracted modes of operation. The landing gear doors are operated hydraulically from the aircraft's onboard system. The landing gear oleo strut is designed to absorb the aircraft's flight loads upon landing and is capable of compressing a full 15 inches in order to facilitate this function. The shock struts are not interchangeable, but still initiate ease of maintainability and durability. A positive down lock mechanism prevents any inadvertent activation of the gear while on the ground.

Catapult Hook

The catapult hook incorporates the use of a forged steel hook for the attachment of the shuttle pendant and holdback cable. The hook attaches to the lower forward fuselage at station 210.8. Access to the hook is initiated through doors located on the bottom of the fuselage through the activation of a button next to those doors. By virtue of the hook's own weight it opens the doors, allowing the hook to be fully extended by hand. However, in order for this sequence of events to occur, the nose wheel and gear must be in the fully lowered position. After catapulting, as the nose gear retracts the hook returns to its original position in the fuselage and is locked into position upon closure of the nose gear wheel well doors.

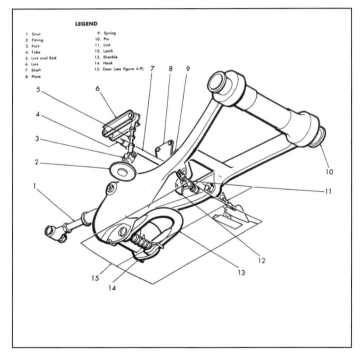

The catapult hooks (2 in all), located near the wing fuselage juncture on both sides of the aircraft, support the catapulting cable, whose attachment to the ram on the hydraulic ram provides the necessary energy for the Cutlass to obtain flight from a short carrier deck. *Courtesy Author*

Nose Gear

The nose gear also incorporates the use of a singular oleo strut primarily constructed from steel, and is activated hydraulically in unison with the main gear. Along with the oleo struts and activating mechanism resides a 24 x 7.7 inch high-pressure tire or wheel, a shimmy damper, and a pre-rotation unit. Air bled from the cockpit pressurizing system is routed to a turbine on the nose gear well via the nose gear strut. Upon activation, the turbine pre-rotates the nose gear wheel before landing, thus significantly increasing the permissible sinking speed of the wheel during contact. The entire nose gear retracts aft and upwards, and securely comes to rest in the nose wheel well located in the underside of the forward fuselage. It also must be stated that the forward wheel well doors, like the main gear doors, are closed when the gear is extended or retracted, only to remain open during the extension or retraction process. A ground lock mechanism also prevents the nose gear from retracting while on the ground.

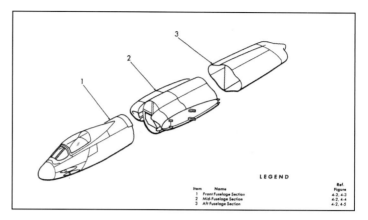

Exploded view of the body clearly outlines the three primary subassemblies comprising the entire fuselage assembly of the F7U-1. *Courtesy Author*

Body Group Overview

The fuselage of the XF7U-1 and F7U-1 are comprised primarily of aluminum alloy, magnesium alloy, stainless steel (aft section), metalite, and fabrilite. Both types of aircraft were assembled employing stressed skin semi-monocoque construction. This also involved reinforced bulkheads stiffened transversely and longitudinally by longerons and stiffening extending from the nose (station −22) to station 184.5. The midsection of the fuselage extends from station 184.5 to station 306.5. The aft section enshrouds both jet engines and starts at station 306.5 to station 449.25. Numerous access panels and doors were made available for the proper servicing and repair of the aircraft.

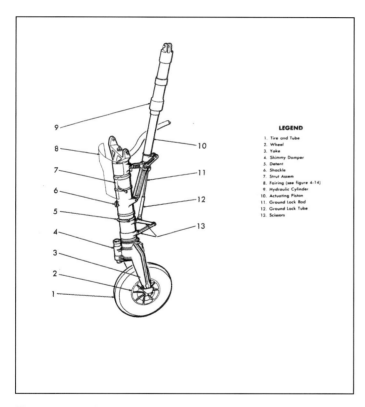

The nose gear oleo strut is rather long and somewhat suggests a lack of strength on its part, and did in fact cause problems in initial flight testing. The reasoning behind its longevity resides in properly alighting the aircraft's angle of attack and best utilizing the aircraft's lift to drag coefficient to obtain maximum lift on take off and landing. *Courtesy Author*

When discussing the fabrication of any semi-monocoque constructed airframe, one must be cognizant of how this process is achieved. Semi-monocoque airframes are constructed in a device known as a jig, whose sole function is to position each of the bulkheads or wing ribs required to generate its respective airframe. Station numbers on drawings show where the bulkheads and wing ribs belong in relation to each other and to the overall length of the aircraft. The stationing numbers show the exact position each specific bulkhead and wing rib belongs on the jig for proper assembly. Every station diagram has a starting point of origin, usually at station 0.00, to the right evoking positive numbers and to the left negative numbers. Each number represents the distance that bulkhead is from the origin in inches.

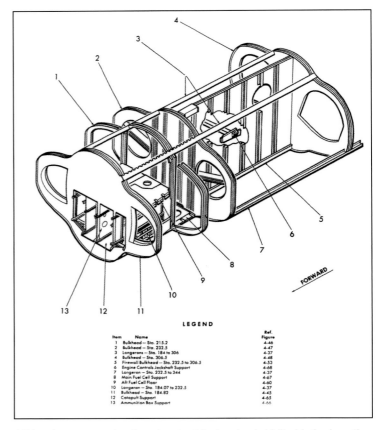

Midsection structural review denotes this structural rigidity. Notice how the structural frame differs from that of the bulkheads. *Courtesy Author*

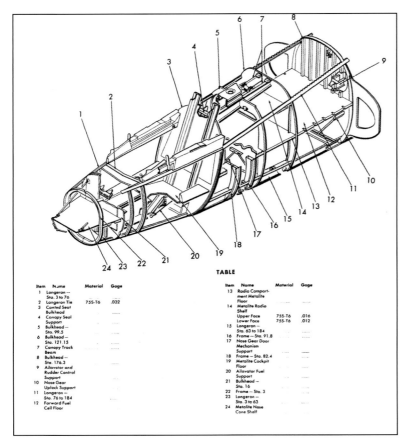

Front fuselage structural subassembly is represented in this picture conveying its light but apparent complexity involved in this design. *Courtesy Author*

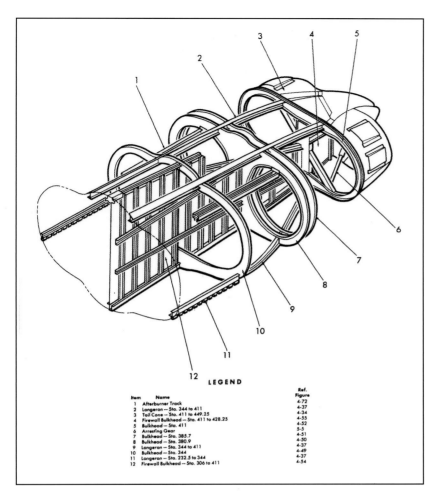

Aft fuselage structural diagram enforces the simple, light, but functionally resilient design of the aircraft. All flight loads transmitted from the wings through the fuselage are reacted smoothly through this design. *Courtesy Author*

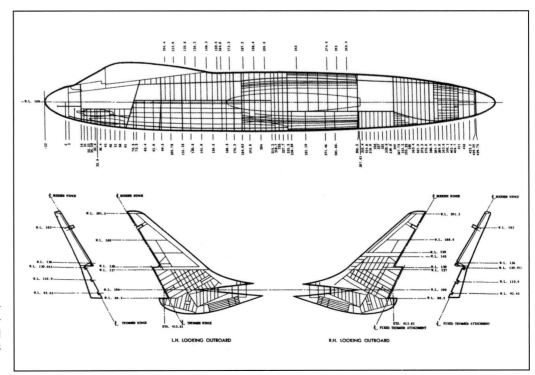

Fuselage and vertical stabilizer stationing diagram exposes the rather simple orderly assembly of all structural components in the fabrication of this vehicle. *Courtesy Author*

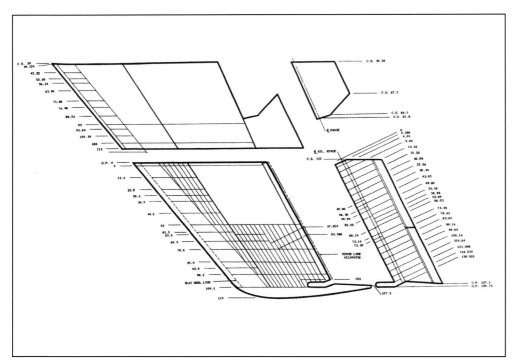

This wing stationing and fabrication drawing functions the same as its fuselage stationing counterpart. All stationing diagrams help in the fabrication of fuselage and wing jigs, facilitating construction of the entire aircraft. *Courtesy Author*

Jig dimensional diagrams determine the key attachment points of all key structural members placed in the jig, facilitating initial assembly of the airframe. *Courtesy Author*

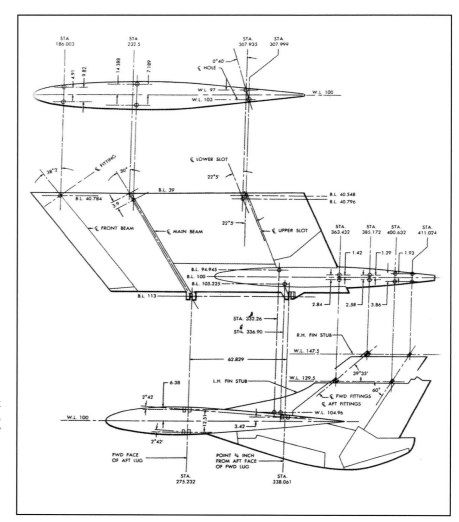

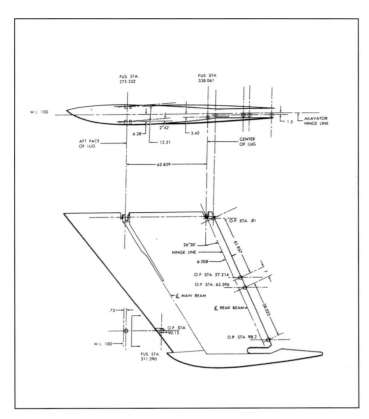

Outer panel wing jig provided the same service in its fabrication. *Courtesy Author*

Longerons

Longeron (stringers) assemblies proliferate along the right and left hand sides, as well as the top and bottom of the fuselage. The upper and lower longerons prorogate from station 3 to that of station 411. The primary bending loads are reacted by these longeron sections. The upper longeron section, located between station 28 and 76.06, supports the cockpit sliding section. The tracts for the canopy are located on top of this structure. The longeron located between stations 120 and 175 and 184.82 and 220 are extended sections containing hinge lobes. These, in turn, mate with holes in similar extrusions that facilitate the removal of the front and aft fuel cell panels.

Bulkheads and Frames

There are five bulkheads that comprise the forward fuselage, four residing in the midsection, and four in the aft section. There are three frames that act as partial bulkheads, reacting to flight loading and providing further fuselage reinforcement. Their respective locations are stations 3, 82.4, and 91.8. Bulkheads, on the other hand, are usually solid in stature (while frames are not) and act as beams, employing stiffened or reinforced webs and flanges. These incremental flanges are usually riveted, or more commonly spot-welded to the fuselage skin panels. Located in the midsection assembly is the firewall bulkhead. It is a stiffened aluminum alloy sheet extending along the fuselage center section from station 232.5 to station 306.5. There is another firewall bulkhead located in the aft section which is stiffened stainless steel extending from station 306.5 along the fuselage centerline to station 428.5.

Several fittings exist attached to the bulkhead that are vital for the complete operation of the aircraft. Located at bulkhead station 232.5 and attached is an aluminum alloy forging necessary for the hoist fitting. The bulkhead at station 161.5 is armour plated and is stiffened by an aluminum alloy web. The barrier guard support fitting is positioned on the forward side of that bulkhead at station 16.

Supports

There are nine structural supports built into the F7U-1 airframe. The first constitutes the nose gear mechanism support located at station 91. It is fabricated from aluminum alloy webs augmented by stiffeners and angles. Next, the canopy seal support is located at station 82 and is constructed of magnesium alloy sheet pan and frames. The nose gear up lock support is located at station 158.5. The ailevator and rudder control support is located between stations 176.3 and 184.07. They are, in turn, constructed from aluminum alloy sheet channels, brackets, and angles. The catapult support is located between stations 184.84 and 215.2. Between stations 215 and 232.5 rests the main fuel cell support, and is also fabricated from aluminum alloy. The engine control jackshaft support and ammunition box support are located between stations 243, 253.5, and stations 184.2 and 215.2. Lastly, the ailevator feel support is located between stations 38 and 65 and is comprised mainly from aluminum alloy extrusions.

Fuselage Skin Plating

Doors and panels are strategically placed throughout the fuselage, providing immediate access to vital aircraft and structural components. The Fuselage Skin Plotting Reference Diagram in Figure 1 outlines the important and relevant panels required for the proper operation and maintenance of the F7U-1 aircraft.

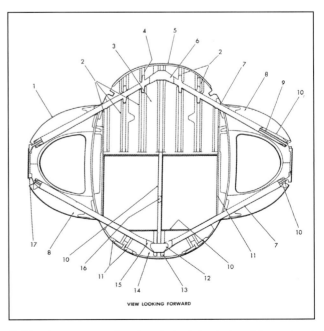

Bulkheads are generally characterized by being fully enclosed, demonstrating the use of structural stiffeners or stringers transversely, traversing the structural component. *Courtesy of Author*

39

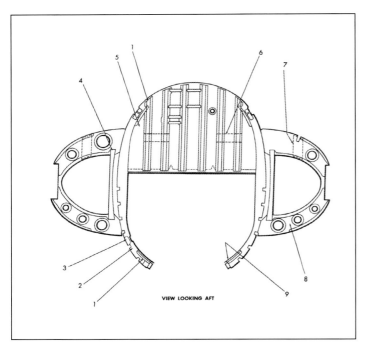

This fuselage bulkhead at station 176.3 displays vertical stiffeners usually spot welded to ease fabrication. Lightening holes are visible, demonstrating how important the reduction of overall weight in the airframe actually is. *Courtesy Author*

Wing Group Overview

The wing of the XF7U-1 and F7U-1 employs the use of fully cantilevered stressed skin construction. The very nature of this method of design and fabrication allows for a replicating center section comprised of aluminum alloy, magnesium alloy, and metalite to support the vertical tail, the main landing gear, and the two outer panels. The removable outer panels consist of both aluminum and magnesium alloys in their principle construction, and also support the outer leading edge slat, wing tip, and the ailevators, which are control surfaces (one per each side of the wing) that combine the function of both elevator and ailerons into one unit. The Cutlass did not use landing flaps, so speed brakes were used to help slow this vehicle's ground speed upon landing. Those speed brakes, located on the wings, extend from the fuselage to wing center section station 88 and are hinged at the rear beam. These brakes are covered with magnesium for ease of strength and durability. Slats located in the wing center and outer section were also fabricated from magnesium.

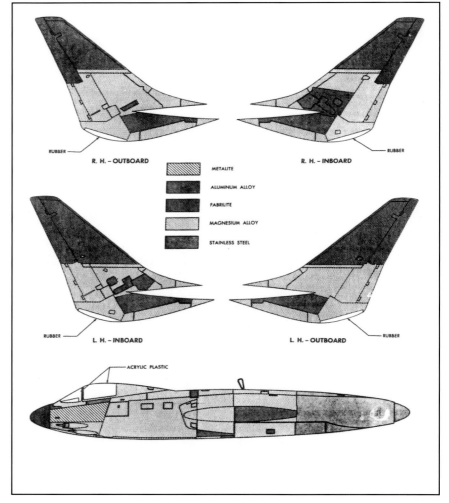

Skin plating diagrams provide intimate knowledge of the material make up of the aircraft. This fuselage plating diagram displays and provides the primary and secondary material used in covering the Cutlass airframe. *Courtesy Author*

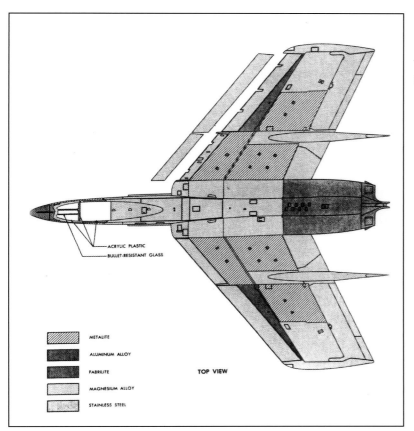

Top view of this F7U-1 reveals variations in skin plating material used. *Courtesy Author*

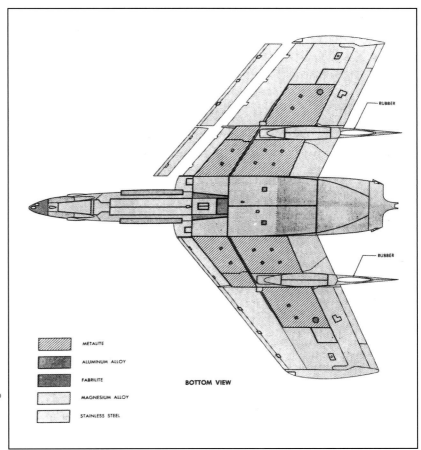

Bottom view depicts the same scenario as the top and fuselage plating diagrams. *Courtesy Author*

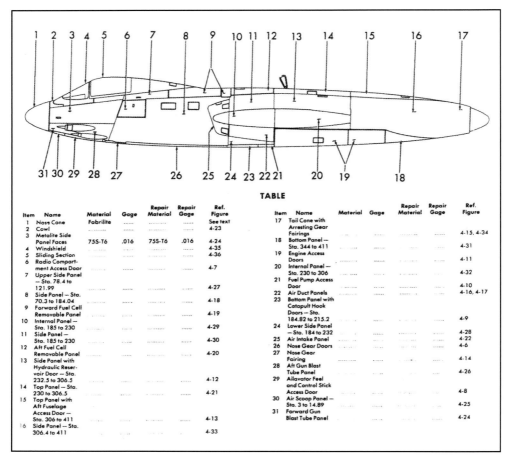

Fuselage plating reference diagram refers to the ordered inclusion of specially contoured and fabricated skin plating. *Courtesy Author*

Wing Group Center Section
The wing center section consists of two panels located and bolted to each side of the fuselage midsection at the front, main, and rear beams. The internal structure employs the use of three beams; two ribs that, in turn, support the main landing gear and wing fold hinge fittings. Also included in this intricate structure reside eleven nose ribs, which are attached to the front beam. This structure utilizes the exclusive use of aluminum, offset by magnesium alloy used for stiffeners and clips. The skin covering from to rear beams and the upper and lower surfaces respectively consists primarily of metalite. An aluminum panel hinge located under the leading edge slats provides access to the surface forward of the front beam. Further access to the two fuel cells and inner structure is achieved by the removal of metalite panels resting on the wing's lower surface.

Wing Beam
The wing's three (front, main, and rear) beams are located in the center section and provide the principle support for the outer panel, the center section leading edge slat, the vertical fins, the air brakes, and the wing fuselage attachment members. The front beam consists primarily of aluminum web and provides the attachment point for the nose ribs and leading edge slats. Holes in the web facilitate access for the slat track and its actuating cylinder. The main wing beam is attached at fuselage station 230.5. This vitally important structural member is an extruded section containing flanges and web and end fittings. Its strength is further enhanced through stiffening by C-section stiffeners. The rear beam attaches to the fuselage at station 307 and is fabricated form sheet webs and cap strips that are necessary in the location of the speed brake hinge fittings and the vertical tail attachment fittings in the inboard rear beams. The web carries the speed brake load while the outboard web, located between center section stations 92 and 108, carries the vertical tail load.

Ribs
The wing center section ribs consist of ten nose ribs securely attached to the front beam. Also, there are two (inboard and outboard) ribs extending from the leading edge to the rear beam. Two of the nose ribs residing at stations 71.68 and 76.98 are equipped with tracks for the slat activating cylinder and roller assembly to operate properly. Additional fittings reside on three more nose ribs located at center stations 52.50, 56.14, and 95.64, and are the guides for the slat. The inboard and outboard ribs are both further divided into three sections delineated by the front and main beams. The aft portions of both ribs are better known

as the landing gear ribs. The main gear forward trunion fitting is mounted between them respectively. The addition of a doubler aft of the main beam bolsters this area's resistance to shear loads. This portion of the outboard rib forward of the front beam is the bulkhead responsible for that transference of the shear load to the nose skin. A slat gap fairing sheet is mounted on the leading edge of the outboard ribs and prevents the inclusion of air into the wing fold cavity upon slat extension.

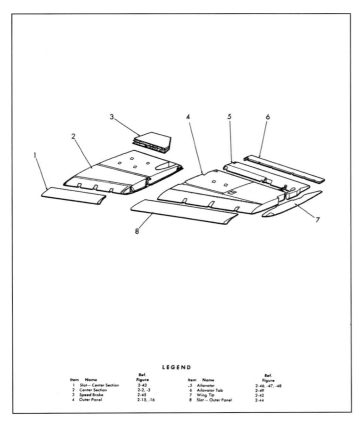

Wing group subassembly breakdown remands the image of functionality and order in its assembly. *Courtesy Author*

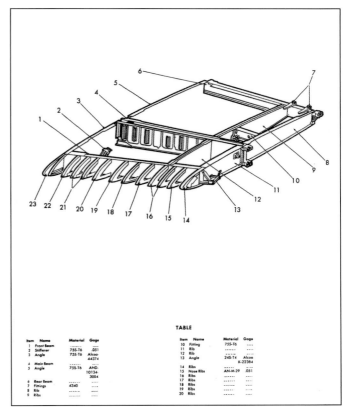

Center section wing structural assembly clearly denotes the wing torque box and wing rib assembly, adding to the static as well as dynamic load integrity of the airframe. *Courtesy Author*

43

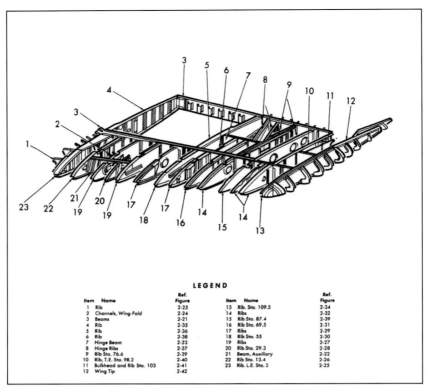

The outer wing panel is structurally endowed, utilizing a outer panel torque box that doubled as a fuel cell enhancement and increased the Cutlass' flight time. *Courtesy Author*

Outer Panel

The outer wing panel, quite simply, is that portion of the wing that extends beyond the wing fold line. Although this panel is slightly tapered, it embraces the same sweep angle as the center section wing portion. A leading edge slat hydraulic activator occupies the leading edge, while the ailevator resides at the trailing edge of that panel. A fuel cell rests between the main and rear beams extending from outer panel stations 3 to 55. Structural skin plating is provided, in part, to generous amounts of magnesium alloy supplemented by copious amounts of metalite. Both main and rear beams are constituted by aluminum alloy further reinforced by two auxiliary beams accentuated by fourteen ribs. Folding of the outer panel is accomplished hydraulically, further reducing the span to approximately 18 feet. This is initiated for adequate aircraft storage aboard the aircraft carrier.

Outer Wing Panel Beams

The major beams (main and rear), accompanied by three auxiliary beams (leading edge auxiliary beam, ailevator control hinge beam, and the wing fold strut channels), constitute the bulk of critical components needed in the outer wing panel's structural definition. There are forged wing hinge fittings to which the center section is attached and, through their union to the upper and lower main beam flanges in conjunction with rear beam and doublers, ensure the proper alignment of the wing's outer panel. A steel pin located in the lower main fitting is hydraulically activated to engage and "lock" or disengage and "unlock" the wing's outer panel for use. In the lock position, or in the unlock position, the outer panel is in full "spread" position, or in the unlock position the panel can be fully folded.

The main beam is reinforced with doublers bolted together at outer panel station 55. Two spliced plates are accompanied by bent angle flanges and cap strips, while the web is reinforced with stiffeners, gussets, and doublers. This all transpires at the juncture of outer panel station 55. The rear beam serves as the attaching member for the ailevator, along with hinge fittings and supports. The ailevator control hinge beam is located in the aft section of the panel behind the main beam between outer panel station 55 and 76.6. The auxiliary beam serves as the attachment member for two small bulkheads mounted on the aft face of the web.

Ailevators

The ailevators are a single pair of control surfaces that are located on the trailing edges of both outer panels. They perform, as previously stated, the function of both elevators and ailerons. Their structure sports outer skins of magnesium alloy reinforced internally by ribs and channels. Four positions supporting hinge fittings located along the outer panel ream beam serve as attachment points for each ailevator.

Wing Tip

The wing tips are nothing more than streamlined fairings attached to the end of both panels at station 109.5. They are exclusively made for each wing panel and are not interchangeable. The wing tips are also fabricated from magnesium alloy bulkheads and stiffeners enclosed by a magnesium alloy skin. The tips house the running lights and outer panel fuel cell vent lines. Attachment of the wing tips to the wings is facilitated by screws.

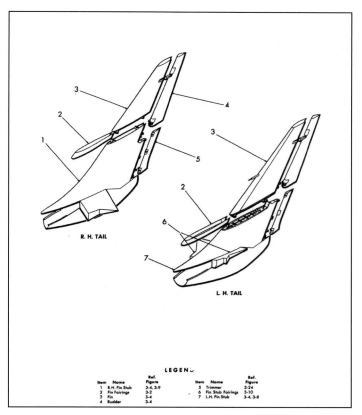

Tail group exploded view reveals the relevant subassemblies required to fabricate the engine tail assembly. *Courtesy Author*

Tail Group

The tail group, in this instance, refers to the twin vertical stabilizers responsible for the lateral stability needed for controlled flight. Incorporated in the designs of both the XF7U-1 and F7U-1, they are mounted on the outboard edges of the wing center section and are comprised of several key structural components. Each stabilizer contains the following elements: an upper fabrilite fin, a lower magnesium alloy fin stub accompanied by its respective wing tie-in fairings and bumper, a fabrilite rudder, and a magnesium built trimmer. The right-hand fabrilite fin houses the radio antenna, only to be offset by the fabrilite constructed left-hand fin in order to eliminate electrical interference.

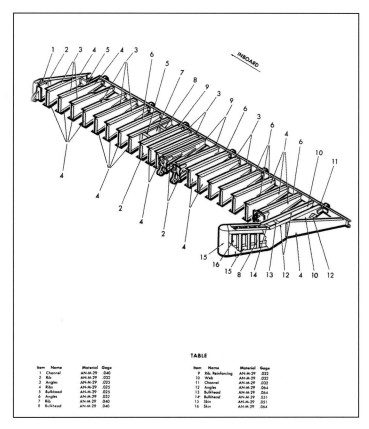

The ailevator structural breakdown, designed as a rather stout, well defined structure to remand the dynamic flight loading encountered by the use of both ailerons and elevator conjointly in this unusual flight control arrangement. *Courtesy Author*

45

The fin on both stabilizers is fabricated from fabrilite (already discussed) to dampen or eliminate any electrical interference usually experienced when using sheet metal. Fin fairings and closing ribs are the only repairable components located in the upper fin assemblies. As far as the closing ribs are concerned, the rib located on the right-hand fin is fabricated from aluminum and exists in three principle web sections reinforced by stiffeners and further stiffened by beads. Both closing ribs are attached to the beam fittings and tied into by aluminum alloy clips. Both stabilizers and fin fairings are fabricated from magnesium alloy sheet accentuated by magnesium alloy doublers and splice plates added for additional strength.

The fin stubs are the main structural components responsible for the support and attachment of the fins, the rudders, and the trimmers, highlighting the construction of both vertical stabilizers. The fin stub assembly contains additional fairings attached to the stub and aft beam of the wing center section. Located below the wing center section is a bumper section and a wheel well section positioned forward of the bumper area on the lower side of the wing center section. Right above the bumper section and located aft of the fin stub rests a fin stub extension.

Magnesium alloy highlights the skin components of the fin stub section. Accented by panels of aluminum alloy, especially within the wing section and wheel well area, the fin stubs' upper inboard and outboard panels are constituted from magnesium alloy and sport both aluminum and magnesium alloy access panels. The rest of the stub utilized aluminum alloy and especially magnesium alloy sheets, .040 and .032 gauge in thickness.

Structurally, the left-hand fin stub is shorter than the right-hand stub, and both employ two main beams (forward and rear) consisting of aluminum alloy reinforced by steel attachment fittings and plates. Aluminum alloy angles, channels, and doublers, along with cap strips, round off this complement of components. Aluminum alloy ribs are located between these beams, further defining the stabilizer's aerodynamic shape. The landing gear wheel well compartment and doors are sculpted form a closing rib, channels, bulkheads, and the landing gear door.

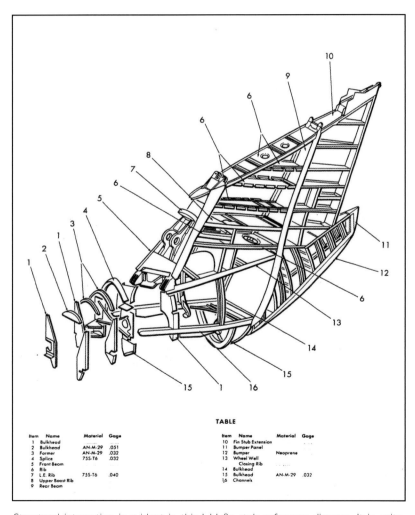

Structural integration is evident in this L.H fin stub reference diagram. It is quite amazing how structurally proficient these subassemblies are, yet maintaining the lightest overall weight. *Courtesy Author*

46

Engine Section

The two engine sections, occupying the aft portion of the fuselage, consist of the right and left hand compartments extending from fuselage station 251.5 to station 411. Access to both engines is granted through engine removal doors and panels located on the underside of the fuselage structure.

Natural engine aspiration is accomplished through air entering the fuselage via two air ducts that exist primarily in two parts, the first of which involves the boundary layer flow originating by the beginning or leading edge of the duct and extending aft along the side of the fuselage to station 222.22. The main duct consists of a fabrilite duct, main beam tie-in duct, coupling assembly, and a duct controller. The fabrilite duct is located between stations 186.5 and 223.88 and operates electrically activated doors. The main beam tie-in ducts, coupling assemblies, and duct controller are located at stations 225.88 to 235.25, 235.25 to 240.15, and station 251.1 respectively. This entire assembly is responsible for the unobstructed subsonic flow required for proper engine operation. Magnesium alloy comprises the bulk of these structures as well.

Fire Seals

Fire seals fabricated from 18-8 stainless steel and located at station 306.5 are attached to each of the engine's combustion chamber sections, separating them from their accessories section and greatly reducing the risk of engine fires.

Engine Supports

Both engines are secured in position through the use of three steel support installations. The first is located in the front of the engine at stations 253.5 and 264, and is further facilitated through the attachment of a steel fin and linkage. The others, forward of the rear beam bulkhead station 306.5, are spring-loaded and hand activated.

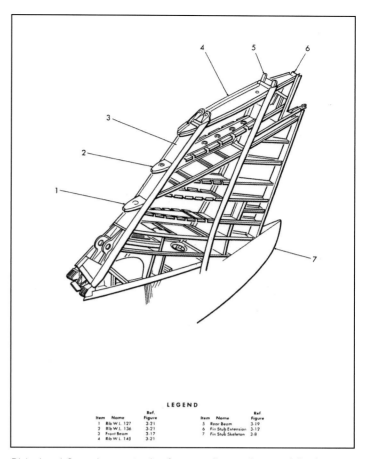

Right hand fin stub structural ref.erence diagram is essentially the same as its left hand counterpart, accentuating this fully functioning structural integration with the emphasis on efficient but lightweight structures. *Courtesy Author*

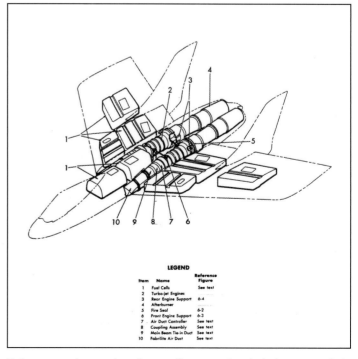

Reference engine section diagram illustrates the dual placement of the engines and fuel storage capacity to feed them. *Courtesy Author*

47

Chapter 4

Westinghouse J34 Turbojet

From the historic first flight of the Wright Brothers in 1903 until the dawn of the jet age, the power plant has limited aircraft in performance. Propeller/piston engines, although declining in overall weight and augmented by appreciable gains in power, nonetheless dashed the hopes of aircraft designers from obtaining truly high-speed aircraft. From the U.S. Navy's perspective, Westinghouse held the most promise for the fledgling turbojet and its subsequent reputation forged upon its newest contender, the 24C, better known as the "J34." Early evaluations of the J34 demonstrated its promising qualities, especially in overall weight and adaptability for operations at high altitudes and speed.

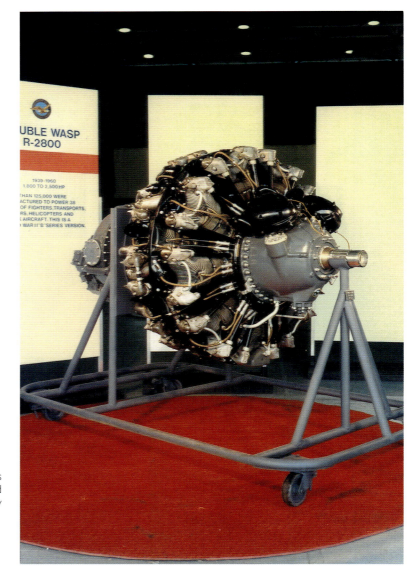

"The engine that won the war" is highlighted in this particular exhibit. The Pratt & Whitney R-2800 represented the summit of piston powered aircraft engines technology circa 1945. *Courtesy of Pratt and Whitney*

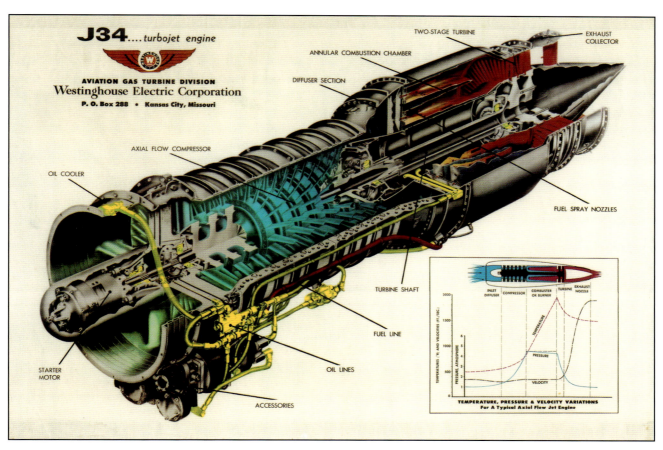

This color cut-a-way represented the future, and in many ways is undeniable in its scope. Westinghouse led the way in the early days of turbojet design and played an important part as a major power broker in this fledging industry. *Courtesy Maurice Smith*

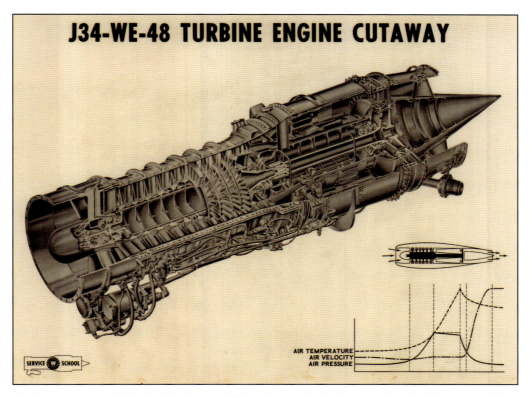

Another cut-a-way of the basic Westinghouse J 34 engine revealing its inner workings. Turbojets, especially the axle flow type, are functionally quite simple and retain large power to weight ratios. *Courtesy Maurice Smith*

Pratt & Whitney first perfected the centrifugal flow turbo jet through their direct copy of the British Nene engine. These units sported copious amounts of "can" combustors arranged in an inclined order around the outer peripheries of the engine frame, connected in turn by a diffuser manifold. *Courtesy Pratt & Whitney*

The J34 is an axial flow turbojet. Suggesting what the name implies, air is ingested through the front, or intake area of the engine, traverses through this unit in an axial, or straight, direction, only to be expelled at the other end at great velocity. This is, of course, not to be confused with a centrifugal flow turbojet. A centrifugal flow turbojet is characterized by its robust appearance. It is best described for its single or double (dual entry) staged impeller, whose sole function is to accelerate the on-coming air in an outward manner, converting the air's kinetic energy to pressure energy entering a diffuser comprised of divergent passages. From here high pressure air enters the combustion chambers to be mixed with fuel, where ignition and combustion takes place. The hot expanding gas exits the chambers and flows through the turbine, initiating rotation. After primary ignition combustion is continuous. The turbine section is connected to the compressor via a shaft. The turbine, in turn, controls the compressor speed. Centrifugal flow turbojets are identified by one, two, or at most three stages, and dictate the very robust nature of the design. This, in many ways, limits the power produced by these engines.

This lonely Pratt & Whitney J42 belongs to a Grumman F9F Panther Jet (foreground), and was extensively used by the U.S. Navy early on in Jet power transition during the late 1940s through early 1950s. *Courtesy Author*

Cut-a-ways are far and few between, but this particular one is of the J42 centrifugal unit. Although quite robust in cross section, it fell from grace as a major contender in the turbojet arena due to that particular design oversight. Producing 8,750 lbs in afterburner for a brief time eclipsed their axle flow counterparts. *Courtesy Pratt & Whitney*

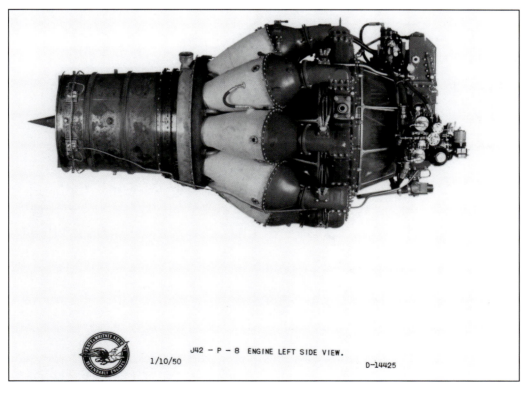

Side view of this J 42 reveals its overall "stoutness" and compact stature. It found its direct design lineage from the Rolls Royce Nene engine, whose basic design architecture is a direct descendent from Sir Frank Whitres' initial work. *Courtesy Author*

Cut-a-ways of Westinghouse J 34s are not readily found, but when they are they are extremely revealing as to their inter working. Clearly seen here is the 11 stage compressor, diffuser section, eventually revealing its single annular combustion chamber and finally its two stage turbine. *Courtesy Author*

The J34's inherent design architecture, on the other hand, provides the room for growth and flexibility needed for this type of turbojet to evolve. Axial flow compressors are smaller in cross section and are accentuated with more stages. Each compressor stage is offset by a stator, or flow straightener, enabling the compression process to take place between each corresponding stage. Like its centrifugal flow predecessor, the hot compressed air enters a diffuser section, quickly diverging the air to a combustion chamber (annular) where fuel is added and ignited. The hot expanding gas exits the chamber and flows through the turbine blades, also initiating rotation. Likewise, the turbine wheel is attached to a shaft connected to the compressor. Early axial flow units usually contained both a low and high-pressure turbine, thus extracting most of the kinetic energy from the hot expanding gas flow.

This J34 is displayed at Drake Field Municipal Airport in Fayetteville, Arkansas. Exposing its compressor section by the removal of its cowling also reveals the starter assembly necessary for the compression process to take place. *Courtesy Maurice Smith*

Maurice Smith, standing next to the J34 cut-a-way, is resting his hand on the elevate stage of the compressor section. The front hub, coaxially mounted by four guide vanes, is responsible for the location of the compressor shaft first bearing. It also houses the starting mechanism and provides energy to the accessories section of the turbojet. *Courtesy Maurice Smith*

From this view it is blatantly apparent how the compressor blades are arranged to enhance maximum mass flow through the engine. The tips of the blade sport localized airfoil shapes to help accelerate the mass flow through the engine. *Courtesy Maurice Smith*

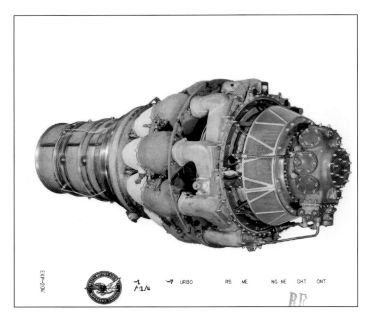

Centrifugal flow units traditionally located their accessories section in the front of the inlet. Also note how the can burners were placed radially around the periphery of the engine frame, each connected to the diffuser manifold. *Courtesy Pratt & Whitney*

Axial flow turbojets demonstrated a 7% higher efficiency in overall pressure range than centrifugal units, which demonstrate high losses due to the higher tip speeds. By their very nature, axial flow turbojets dictate higher mass flows than their centrifugal flow counterparts. In essence, a centrifugal flow unit would have to be 80% larger in cross section to maintain the same mass flow rate of a corresponding axial flow unit. Because of the robustness involved with centrifugal turbojets, this limited its use to high sub-sonic and transonic aircraft designs due to too much induced aerodynamic drag.

The J34's smaller diameter and cross sectional areas enabled aircraft designers to craft and finely tailor airframes to meet with smaller fineness ratios (fuselage width/fuselage length), thus producing low drag airframes at which higher transonic and supersonic speeds could be achieved.

Design Principles
Symbols:
W_q = free air used in propulsion-pounds per second.
W_f = fuel and mass carried in airframe pounds per second.
g = acceleration of gravity feet per second^2.
C = jet velocity relative to airframe feet per second, or jet velocity relative to ground + flight velocities.
V = flight velocity – feet per second.
H_F = heating value of fuel (lower value usually used) in British thermal units (BTUs).
J = mechanical equivalent of heat.

The J34's operation relies upon the force required to accelerate the air through the engine and its reaction to the force, principally in the opposite direction. This reaction is called thrust, and is transmitted to the housing of the engine. Its direction is diametrically opposed to that of the ensuing airflow. The magnitude of the thrust equals the mass flow (weight of air being ingested, lb/sec) of the accelerated gas times its overall change in velocity:

Net thrust (mass x change of velocity) = $W_A(c-v)/g$.

When compared to a piston/propeller engine combination, a propeller accelerates a large mass of air to allow for velocity, while an axial flow gas turbine accelerates a smaller mass to a far greater velocity.

The increase in flight speed does not enact an overall decrease or change in velocity to the gas transiting through the engine. In fact, when additional air is rammed into the engine the product of mass flow and velocity change decreases slightly. Therefore, in regard to a turbojet engine, and axial flow in particular, thrust is almost independent of flight speed. Thrust horsepower available varies as a linear function in relation to that of flight speed:

Thrust Power (thrust x flight speed) = $W_A(c-v)V/550g$.
Jet Power (mass x velocity squared) = $W_A(C^2-V^2)/Zg\,550$
Propulsion Efficiency (thrust power / jet power) = $2V/C+V$.
Overall Efficiency (thrust power / fuel input power) = $W_AV(c-v)/gJW_FH_F$.

Contrasting the thrust horsepower available for a piston/propeller engine is constant power over its aircraft's flight envelope. Likewise, a turbojet may be considered a constant thrust engine. Table 4-1 reveals the differences between these two types of power plant as understood some sixty-four years ago.

It can be seen why centrifugal flow units would have trouble ingesting airflow to the same ratio as their axial flow counterparts. *Courtesy Author*

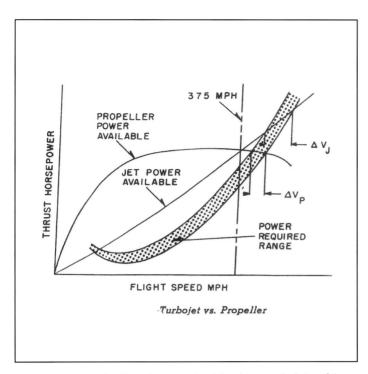

From simple inspection it can be ascertained that jet propelled aircraft have a definite advantage in speed, power, and overall efficiency beyond flight speeds of 375 mph. This is due to the newly introduced presence of axial flow turbojets. They did, however, suffer from delayed response and took more time to power up at low airspeeds in their infancy. *Courtesy Author*

By simple inspection of figure 4-1, it should be apparent that the top speed of a turbojet-powered aircraft should be greater. The turbojet-powered aircraft is influenced more by drag changes than that of its propeller driven counterpart. This is evident by the position of V_j (velocity of jets) to V_p (velocity of propeller) on the table. Although for flight speeds below 375 mph propeller driven aircraft demonstrate their prowess, beyond this speed the turbojet is superior.

Fuel Consumption
Turbojets in their infancy were notoriously inefficient and extremely thirsty. In fact, propeller/piston powered aircraft possessed a 40% greater endurance than turbojet powered aircraft of similar size and weight. Not until the introduction of the dual spool (split compressor; i.e. J57) did fuel efficiencies improve significantly. Today's turbo fan engines are the pinnacle of design efficiency, but the year was 1945, and things were much different. Specific fuel consumption for an axial flow gas turbine at that time would register a resounding 1.25 lb. of fuel per hr per lb thrust (sea level conditions). By today's standards, specific fuel consumption dwells around .4 lb fuel per hour per lb thrust. It is apparent that we had a long way to go. However, back in 1945 the Westinghouse J34 presented the summit of gas turbine technology:

Fuel Input Power (fuel flow x fuel heating value) – W_F x H_F x J/550.

The J34 Turbojet Engine: Operational Overview
The J34 engine is, basically, an internal combustion gas turbine power plant predicated upon the Bryton Cycle.

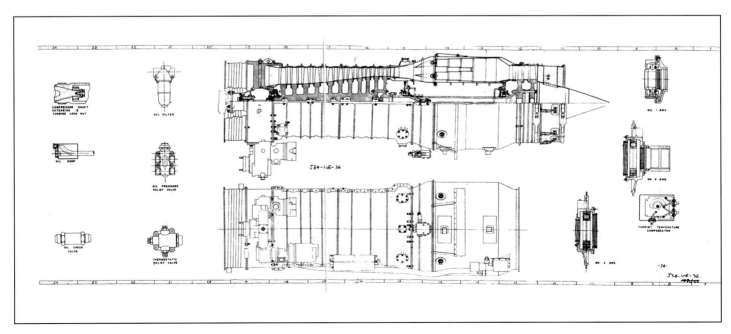

This factory drawing of a J34 denotes all eleven compressor stages, as well as the diffuser and annular combustion chamber. The 2 stage turbine can also be viewed. Note the lean features, fortifying its overall efficient design architecture. *Courtesy Author*

This design consists of an axial flow eleven stage compressor delivering a resounding 50 lb/sec mass flow and a pressure ratio of 3.65:1—extremely impressive even for 1945 standards. Incorporated in the three-way diffuser located directly behind the compressor resides the fuel manifold, employing 60 spray nozzles. Upon fuel delivery in the double annular combustion chamber combustion is therefore initiated, resulting in the instantaneous expansion of hot gas. This gas flows through the two-stage turbine, exiting through a fixed area exhaust nozzle. Other lesser known elements of this engine would incorporate the accessories section, which consists of the fuel control, oil pump, tachometer, hydraulic pump, and generator. All subsequent energy required to power these accessories is facilitated through suitable reduction gearing from the engine rotor (compressor). The lubrication system exists in a "dry sump" system involving the use of solid oil lubrication. A six-unit type gear pump employing one pressure and five scavenge elements provides oil at 80 psi.

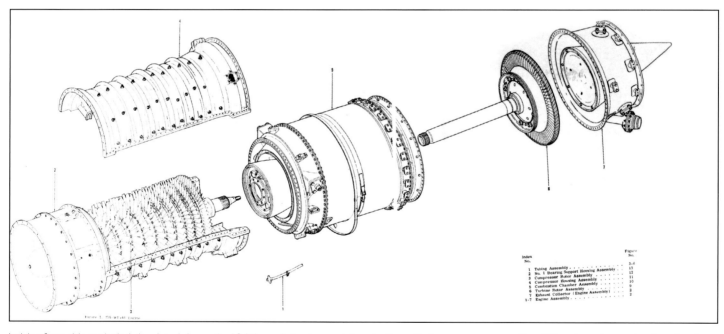

Judging from this exploded view breakdown, the J 34 through 4 subassemblies, starting with the compressor section diffuser/annular combustion chamber, turbine assembly and tail cone, one can appreciate its functional simplicity. *Courtesy Author*

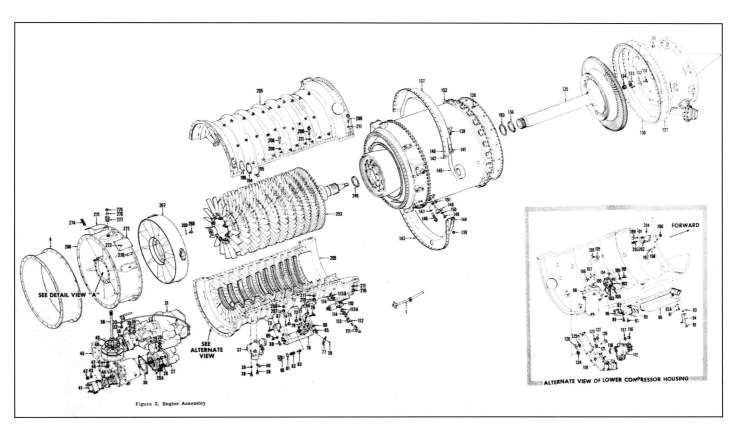

Another exploded view, this time including the accessories section. *Courtesy Author*

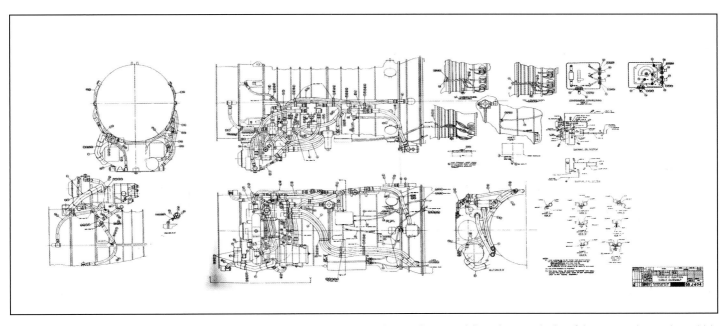

J 34 engineering drawings are hard to come by, but provide an essentially basic understanding, especially as the complexity of the accessories section, which govern the fuel, engine temperature, and rpm in the successful operation of the power plant. *Courtesy Author*

Air enters the front of the engine and passes through the helical-wound oil cooler and front bearing support coaxially positioned by the inlet guide vanes. From here the airflow is compressed to roughly 4 atmospheres while en transit through the 11-stage compressor. Lastly, at the end of the compressor flow path are positioned the straightening vanes, whose sole purpose is to give the air exiting the compressor an axial direction into the diffuser.

Next, the hot compressed air enters an all stainless steel, three-way diffuser, dividing the airflow to an annular combustion chamber. The air, radially passing through both walls of this type of combustor through carefully selected hole sizes in the wall between liners, insures proper cooling and the stability of the combustion process over a wide range of altitudes and flight speeds. The fuel manifold located in the front of the combustor, through the combined usage of sixty spray nozzles, is responsible for the introduction of fuel into the combustion chamber.

The temperature of the exiting gas mandates the limiting factors in engine operation due to the high temperature effects of the expanding gas on the turbine blades. The two-stage turbine extracts enough energy from the hot gases passing through to drive the compressor and its accessories section. The turbine utilizes roughly 75% of the power developed in the combustion chamber. Maximum operating conditions demand approximately 10,000 horsepower to drive the compressor. In comparison, one single turbine blade traveling at 12,500 rpm produces more horsepower than an automobile engine circa 1945.

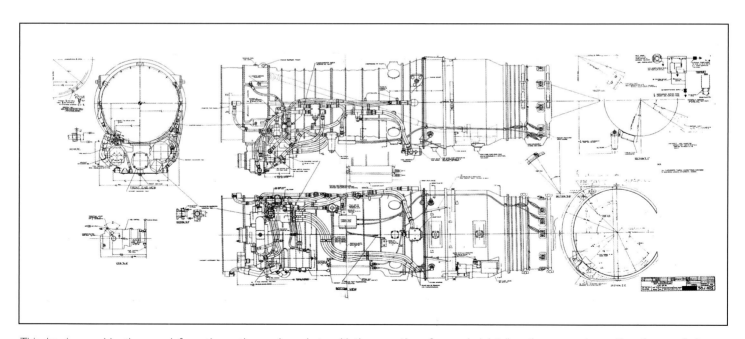

This drawing provides the same information as the previous photo with the exception of expanded detail on the accessories section. *Courtesy Author*

The accessories section can be observed in lesser detail, suggesting an earlier J 34 model. This particular turbojet powered the McDonnell F 3H-2 Banshee. *Courtesy Author*

Annular combustion chambers are used in the J 34 (one per turbojet), connecting to the diffuser inlet. The three tier combustor allows cooling air to flow between baffles via special cooling holes drilled in these subsequent baffles. *Courtesy Author*

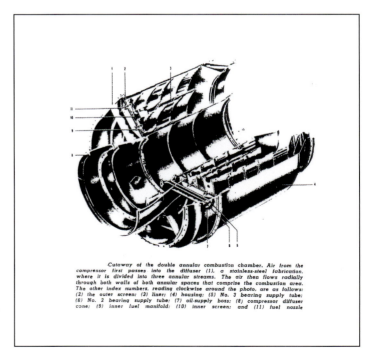

Hot expanding gas flow exits the rear of the engine via the 2 stage turbine and tail cone. *Courtesy Author*

Downstream from the turbine, the gas flows through a stainless steel fabricated exhaust collector. The flow is then accelerated through a conical exhaust nozzle by the restriction in area of the nozzle. Exit velocities of the gas are welled around 1200 feet per second, the reaction of which provides the engine's propulsive thrust.

Attachment points are located along its long, slender frame. Two trunnions are located on the diffuser housing. These particular attachments are responsible for accepting fore and aft loading, side loading, and part of the vertical load. The third attachment point can be found toward the front end of the engine, located on the cast front bearing support. This joint is of universal design and accepts the vertical loads only, while permitting axial expansion of the engine and distortion of the airframe taking place between the diffuser and the front bearing support without imposing additional loads on the engine.

It is hard to imagine that a machine as involved as a turbojet could possess a single rotating assembly—the compressor. This device is of axial flow design, its shaft extending through the center of the combustion chamber, and is firmly attached to the two-stage turbine on the other side. The compressor assembly is supported on three bearings. The first, located coaxially in the inlet guide vanes, is responsible for accepting all the thrust loads incurred by this rotational element. The other two are roller bearings, and are principally located at the down stream end of the compressor and the other upstream from the two-stage turbine. This type of bearing permits axial expansion from the rotating parts relative to the stationary components. The need to keep engine components strong, but light, is paramount in turbojet design. Light aluminum and magnesium alloys are employed wherever practical, while the thickness of ferrous metals are kept to a minimum in conjunction with adequate safety factors and load limits.

Oil Cooler

The oil cooler is the most forward located component on the engine casing. It is fabricated from rectangular helical wound aluminum tubing. The lubricating oil en route to the engine bearing must first pass through this area, allowing the cooling effect from the incoming air to take place. This cooling unit is bolted to the front flange of the cast magnesium inlet-bearing support. This casing is comprised of an inner and outer cylindrical shell joined by four equally spaced radial struts. The primary function of the inner cylinder is to provide bearing support for the front of the compressor shaft and also to locate the engine starter. A shaft located in the lower radial support drives the accessories section gearbox.

Rear view of the J 34 sports both 2 stage turbine and tail cone. The turbine extracts roughly 75% of the energy from the gas flow exiting through the cone. *Courtesy Maurice Smith*

Ten of the eleven stages of the axial flow compressor rest on an aluminum spindle to which a steel disc is attached and completes the eleventh stage. The rotating compressor blades, consisting of 12% chrome steel, are located and secured in the outer periphery of the discs by a U-shaped bent wire arrangement. Its very shape enables it to fit into a drilled hole in the spindle grove. This prevents the wire from moving while the blade is positioned over it upon bending the wires against the blade root, locking the blade in position. Stationary compressor blades, or stators, are fabricated from steel and are positioned in grooves machined in the aluminum semi-circular housings. The strators are locked in position by radial screws attached to holes drilled in the housing.

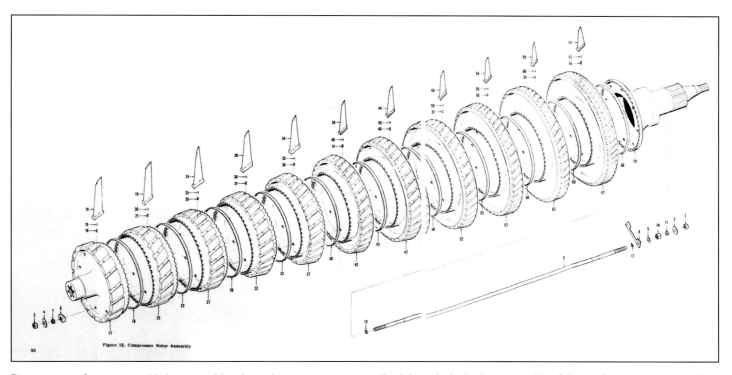

Eleven stages of compressor blades, comprising the entire compressor, are realized through the intricate assembly of that shaft, stage by stage and by interlocking these blades to each hub stage, thus completing the entire assembly. *Courtesy Author*

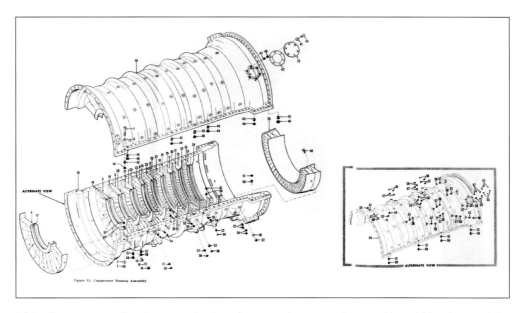

J 34 split compressor housing not only places its respective stators, but provides additional strength in the transference of loads, both thermal and mechanical alike, through this housing via engine attachment points. *Courtesy Author*

This solar afterburner was used in the XF7U-1 and F7U-1, and also powered Vought's F6U-1 Pirate to no avail. Westinghouse would proceed with their own factory produced afterburners featured in the J46-WE-8B engines. *Courtesy Steve Ginter*

Afterburner

The XF7U-1 and F7U-1 Cutlass incorporates the use of a solar equipped afterburner similar to the A-103B model used on the F6U Pirate. On a larger note, the F7U Cutlass celebrated being the first operational U.S. Naval jet aircraft to use afterburners. Afterburners are thrust augmentation devices consisting of a jet pipe attached to the exhaust section downstream on the J34. These jet pipes (as they are known) and one per turbojet are comprised of copious amounts of monel and inconel-x, nickel alloy for high strength at extreme temperatures.

The afterburner's sole function is to increase the overall thrust output from the turbojet by a margin of 30 to 50 percent. Because they burn fuel excessively afterburners are used sparingly. Afterburning is achieved through the introduction of fuel downstream of the turbine exhaust outlet and, when ignited, provides the added thrust desired. Further substantiating this, the area is narrowed at the exhaust-afterburner junction, further diffusing the flow for the eventual inclusion of fuel. Air in the exhaust flow entering the afterburner jet pipe exists in a roughly 60:1 ratio (60 parts air to one part exhaust gas). The advent of a fuel gutter strategically positioned in the afterburner adequately supports combustion. Upon ignition, the gas flow entering the afterburner pipe can be accelerated from 1,200 feet per second to 1,600 feet per second:

P_1 = jet pipe (afterburner) pressure.
P_2/P_1 = turbine pressure ratio.

When afterburner mode is selected fuel sprayed from the fuel gutter is ignited, thus resulting in an increase in jet pipe pressure P_1, and thus influencing the pressure P_2/P_1 ratio across the turbine, and is maintained by the proper positioning of the variable nozzle area from the afterburner section.

Thrust Increase

The increase in thrust brought about by afterburning depends exclusively upon the ratio of the absolute jet pipe temperature before, and after, the inclusion of fuel is burned. Gas temperatures of the J34 hover around 920°K before afterburning, while afterburning temperatures peak out at 1500°K, thus establishing a temperature ratio of 1500°K/920°K = 1.62. The velocity of the jet stream increases as the square root of the temperature ratio $\sqrt{1.62} = 1.25$, therefore placating exhaust velocities up to and beyond 1,600 feet per second.

Chapter 5

Flight Test XF7U-1 and F7U-1

All three XF7U-1 prototypes were assigned Bu Nos. 122472, 122473, and 122474 respectively, and were produced at Vought's Connecticut plant. All other Cutlass derivatives would be produced at Vought's new Dallas, Texas, plant. All three examples would be barged to the Naval Air Test Center at Patuxent River, Maryland, the first of which arrived in September 1948. Test flight and evaluation would soon begin without the use of solar afterburners.

First flight took place 29 September 1948 with Robert Baker at the controls, producing a rather uneventful flight. This first Cutlass (Bu No. 122472) was configured with two instrumentation booms, one on each wing tip, and had to be retrofitted, resulting in one boom being located in the nose of the aircraft due to severe vibration experienced on subsequent flights by Mr. Baker. Number one and Number three Cutlass were soon to be fitted with their solar afterburners in early 1949. Upon completion of this task both examples were sent to Carswell AFB in Fort Worth, Texas, for eight more months of testing, culminating with the completion of this program at a former AFB in Ardmore, Oklahoma, and with flight-testing proceeding quite well. As previously stated, this prompted the Navy to immediately order nineteen new airframes of the next variant, F7U-1, but this was quickly reduced to only 14 examples soon after.

XF7U-1 BuNo 122472 is being barged from Vought's Connecticut plant to the Naval Air Test Center (NATC) at Patuxent River, Maryland. It arrived in early September 1948 for immediate testing. *Courtesy Tom Cathcart*

XF7U-1 No. 472 (short for 122472) began its vigorous test flight program on 29 September 1948 with Robert Baker at the controls. *Courtesy Tom Cathcart*

XF7U-1 No.472, shown here in level flight sporting its twin instrumentation booms, which were immediately replaced upon encountering intense vibrations at high indicated airspeeds. *Courtesy Tom Cathcart*

As for the second Cutlass Bu No. 122473, it met with some harsh and unforgiving events. On 18 February 1949 test pilot William Millar, upon returning from an earlier test flight, experienced a landing gear malfunction precipitating a belly landing, reeking havoc on the nose as well as the main wheels.

XF7U-1 No.473 at Pax River NATC, early 1949. Note the repositioned instrumentation boom on the nose of the aircraft. No further vibrations were encountered. *Courtesy National Naval Aviation Museum*

It took as much as thirteen days to repair the resulting damage, only to meet with certain disaster on a subsequent flight. In fact, on 14 March 1949, after a brief check ride test pilot Millar flew No. 473 on a photo shoot. He was never seen again, with only scant parcels of wreckage found a month later in Chesapeake Bay laying in testimony to his ultimate fate.

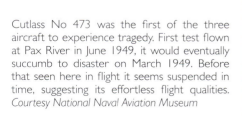

Cutlass No 473 was the first of the three aircraft to experience tragedy. First test flown at Pax River in June 1949, it would eventually succumb to disaster on March 1949. Before that seen here in flight it seems suspended in time, suggesting its effortless flight qualities. *Courtesy National Naval Aviation Museum*

Meanwhile, testing would begin at Croswell and Ardmore AFB with Cutlass 472 and 474, culminating in the discovery of 51 overall deficiencies on the vehicle and the solution to these shortcomings as to how they would apply to the next derivative, the F7U-1. Vought Engineering Memo EM 1140 can be viewed for inspection in Appendix 1.

This report chronicles all 51 deficiencies and their detailed corrective actions as it related to the F7U-1 and eventually the F7U-3. It will be discussed to some extent in a summary located at the end of this chapter.

Initial testing proved that both rudders were required in the overall lateral and longitudinal stability of the aircraft, and some lengthening would be required to eliminate the vehicle's tendency to snake or weave in horizontal flight. Test results also recommended the widening or increase in thickness of the trailing edge of the ailevators from one to four inches. This would eventually be utilized in the F7U-3 production version.

One such test involving Cutlass No. 472, and at the hands of Vought's chief test pilot Paul Thayer, proved rather distressing, if not disastrous, with the pilot narrowly cheating death with only minor medical attention required.

This example, fitted with a dummy 250-gallon wing tank to test the aerodynamic influences on this configuration in regards to the F7U-1, would conclude at the end of the runway. Paul Thayer attempted such a takeoff in this configuration and, upon rotation, experienced his craft starting to yaw and roll. Immediately depressing the rudder peddles to compensate only exasperated the situation even further. His control system, equipped with a new differential rudder, only achieved 50% of full deflection, which had little effect countering this condition. His aircraft settled back on the runway, instantaneously shearing off the landing gear and initiating the entire aircraft to cartwheel. The vehicle quickly broke in two at the air intakes, with the wing and engine section sliding past the cockpit to Mr. Thayer's amazement.

Meanwhile, after this traumatic incident Mr. Thayer did exceed the sound barrier in Cutlass No. 474. He did so by placing his craft in a shallow dive. This is the first naval aircraft to covet this distinction. Thayer, not one to shirk in his responsibilities, would be the provider of another Cutlass first.

While participating in a flight exhibition in the last Cutlass No. 474 at Patuxent River on 7 July 1950 he performed a high-speed, low-level pass. Upon climbing a tremendous fireball erupted in the afterburner section of the Cutlass, forcing Thayer to eventually eject. Not a willing participant at first to use the Vought produced ejection seat, he coaxed his disabled vehicle to nose over, where he could fall from the cockpit through the open canopy. That did not happen, resulting in a full ejection sequence to be initiated, thus saving his life. As he parachuted to a safe landing in the river, he was then hastened to the admirable stand and asked by the announcer, "What will you do for an encore Mr. Thayer?" As for the third Cutlass prototype, its usefulness soon expired upon impact, culminating in a huge fireball on an island located on the Patuxent River.

It is believed that a diaphragm pipe failed in the afterburner section due to the flight loading experienced upon vertical pull out of the high speed pass. It is sad that such a becoming aircraft should meet with such an untimely end without serving their purpose and providing much useful data for the continuation of the program. Carrier suitability tests would soon begin in earnest with the next derivative, F7U-1.

Carrier suitability tests began with F7U-1 No. 124415 from 24 June 1950 to 14 August 1951. With engine developmental problems crippling the testing program Westinghouse J34-WE-34 turbojets were substituted in lieu of the malfunctioning J34-WE-32 with afterburning jets. Because the use of afterburners was circumvented, an additional 1245 lbs. of ballast was added to maintain proper aerodynamic balance of the aircraft. Preparation for carrier suitability trials began with first endorsement from BUAIR restd. letter AER-DE-232, serial number 27199, of 10 April 1950. The rest of this request is stated in the following letter:

From: Bureau of Aeronautics Representative, Dallas, Texas.
To: Chance Vought Aircraft.
Subj: Contract No. a(S)9937, Model F7U-1 airplane: carrier-suitability tests and instrumentation therefore.
Ref: (a) CVA restr ltr X-775 of 16 March 1950 with bar end 1 of 24 March 1950.

This letter outlining the initial provisions for preparing F7U-1 Bu No. 124415 with the proper and subsequent instrumentation needed for the soon approaching carrier suitability tests. General provisions requested would include.

1. Outfitting F7U-1 No. 124415 with dual catapult hook arrangement.

2. In order to comply to addendum No. F7U-1 to SK-38, for 50 percent of the limit on sinking speed for approaches shall be achieved at least 12 times or the limit sinking speed shall be obtained once.

3. The instrumentation of F7U-1 124415 is satisfactory but should be discussed with the instrumentation branch at NATC.

4. Test firing of the four 20mm cannon shall be performed on the 5th plane in lieu of the first.

5. The rest of the letter stipulated when and where structural, static, and carrier arrestor gear evaluation would take place.

Cutlass No 474, shown here in overall Navy blue airframe with natural metal in the afterburner section, along with the landing gear. The nose flash (instrumentation boom included) is yellow and accented by a red diamond. This port side view provides the reader with a clearer understanding of what design elements were embraced. *Courtesy National Naval Aviation Museum*

Meanwhile, Vought's test pilot, W. P. Thayer, had the further distinction of flying the first production example (124415) on 1 March 1950 at Hensley Field, Dallas. After undergoing meticulous scrutiny, F7U-1 124415 would eventually be flown and turned over to the experimental section for further tests in lieu of its acceptance by Patuxent River NATC. Instrumentation installation was completed on aircraft 124415 on 6 July 1950 and it was readied for further testing.

Many pilots, in spite of the abhorrent reputation then developing against the Cutlass and its overall operational qualities, held it high in their regard. This attitude is evident through correspondence to Mr. J. J. Hospers from pilot B. T. Guyton on 25 April 1950. He states the following:

F7U-1 No. 415, the first flight production example of the initial 14 is shown here in flight over NATC Pax River circa 1950. *Courtesy National Naval Aviation Museum*

> The writer (B. T. Guyton) was recently able to obtain a fight in F7U-1 airplane, Bureau Number 124416. During this flight, which was of extremely short duration (35 minutes), the airplane was ferried from Hensley Field to Ardmore under somewhat restricted weather conditions. Due to the fact that overcast prevented evaluating the airplane at high altitudes and high mach numbers, no useful information can be provided on that score. The flight was continued from takeoff to landing at altitudes below 8,000 ft. and the highest mach number obtained was .73.

The underside of 415 is shown with copious amounts of stainless steel employed in the aft fuselage. Many test flights and instrumentation installation took place before carrier suitability trails began in July 1951. *Courtesy National Naval Aviation Museum*

No 415 shown here in a steep bank. Pay particular attention to its inordinately clean aerodynamic lines, a definite plus throughout its revealed experimental career. *Courtesy National Naval Aviation Museum*

He further states:

Several characteristics stood out in regard to flying the F7U airplane which the writer feels worthy of serious consideration for the best means of promoting the Cutlass to the Bureau, various staffs, and fleet operational pilots. It is recommended that we emphatically point up the ease of flying, excellent stall, low speed approach and landing characteristics, and the good ground handling qualities of this airplane.

The writer feels that the reasons for using this approach in placing the F7U before all parties concerned in the best light possible are several. First, since the advent of the F4U-1 type airplane, nearly 10 years ago, Vought has been conceded a company which can provide an excellent high performance airplane but one which is generally more difficult to fly at or near stalling speeds, during take-offs, during approaches to and carrier landings, and during normal field landings. Our accident rate has been high. While we eventually erased the poor landing qualities of the F4U airplane during actual carrier landings, spin-stall and landing accidents have continued to prove embarrassing.

Mr. Guyton further remarks:

The F7U airplane, as judged by this pilot's 35 minute first flight impression and as compared with the F2H-1 and F6U-1 airplanes, has exactly the opposite stall, low speed and landing characteristics from those which were in evidence in the F4U type. The F7U is exceptionally easy to fly, is solid directionally, laterally, and longitudinally in a slow speed approach for and during a landing. The pilot feels at home in this airplane after a brief flight. As Commander C. Gibson said, "After my second flight I was ready to take it aboard any time."

It is to be noted that the writer's (BT Guyton) comments are based on a quick impression after the briefest flight in the F7U-1 airplane; however, it is felt in this case that this impression lends credence to the thought that the F7U-1 airplane starts out in life as a pilot's flying machine as far as low speed operation is concerned. Since one of the Navy's prime interest is to have such advanced airplanes as the F7U type ready for quick adaptation by inexperienced and short time pilots, it is considered that we should capitalize on this and plug the point for all it is worth.

Another point worthy of consideration arose when a recent hydraulic failure in flight left pilot Houser flying F7U-1 Bu No. 124416 at approximately 150 knots IAS with one slat fully extended and one side fully retracted. Little or no lateral trim change was observed! Needless to say this is a highly desirable characteristic.

Mr. Guyton concludes:

It is considered that the additional factor of an "unrestricted" airplane, as far as mach number is considered, which is the probability where the F7U-3 is concerned, gives us an even more saleable article. It is felt by the writer that the F7U airplane with the merit of exceptionally high performance and ease of flying, provides for an excellent selling campaign.

Disaster came beckoning once more and on 6 July 1950 test pilot Warren P. Smith would lose his life at the hands of aircraft 124416. During a landing approach Mr. Smith's craft suffered a massive hydraulic control system malfunction spelling doom for himself and his aircraft.

Immediately after this unfortunate event occurred, the grounding of all active F7U-1 articles took place, placing the entire program in limbo. A subsequent investigation revealed the cause of the accident. A part of the automatic changeover system, activated prematurely due to low hydraulic pressure encountered, caused a control loss thus insuring Mr. Smith's fate. Through correspondence from Paul S. Baker dated 18 July 1950 to Mr. L. S. Hobbs, vice President of Vought lends a greater understanding of the problem as well as arriving at a solution is achieved.

Mr. Baker states:

The situation in connection with the accident to the F7U-1 airplane down here has not changed substantially since I talked to you on the phone last Friday, except that our people, Messrs Clark and Schoolfield, were well received in the Bureau yesterday and our explanation of the accident appears to be accepted. In the meantime I have put together a story of the accident for the information of our people, and a copy is enclosed. The action to be taken as a result of the discussion with the Bureau is as follows:

(1) Airplane to be placarded against extending slats before the landing gear is down and against extending either at excessive speed, and with instructions to set the trim tabs at 10° for landing and takeoff.
(2) The fuel system timing operation is to be checked.
(3) The hydraulic tank capacity is to be increased.
(4) A pressure-operated valve to cut off flow to the auxiliary services when the system pressure falls below a critical valve is to be installed.
(5) Tolerances on the boost cylinder bypass valves are to be tightened.
(6) Changeover spring is to be strengthened.

All of the above are needed to unground the #1 airplane now at Patuxent. We are working on schedule to accomplish this work by the 27th of this month. Certain other changes are contemplated for the other airplanes, such as provision of automatic air bleeders and a hydraulic pump warning light system.

There is very little additional news on the Patuxent accident. The most up-to-date summary is given in the enclosed memorandum of Townsend.

Many tests flights took place at Pax River NATC on Cutlass 415 to ready this test example for its carrier suitability tests in July 1951. *Courtesy National Naval Aviation Museum*

The letters "FT" painted on the nose of 415 denote flight test. Different combinations of test instrumentation were embraced, rounding out the program's agenda. *Courtesy National Naval Aviation Museum*

F7U-1 415 shown at Pax River NATC August 1950, undergoing either an engine maintenance inspection or power plant change. For this model Cutlass engine access was obtained through the aircraft's underside, a design flaw later rectified on the F7U-3 model.
Courtesy National Naval Aviation Museum

Roughly a month later aircraft testing would be reinstated. A second fatality occurred the next month when Chief Test Pilot William Harrigan drowned after the third aircraft ran off the runway into Mountain Creek Lake. His death was attributed to anoxia. Unencumbered by these events testing continued. Many flights accompanied with numerous minor design changes would result. Some of the changes would consist of the following:

(A) The arresting and catapulting equipment would be modified for strength as well as practicality.

(B) The nose gear oleo strut was extended to 12°10' from 8° 52'.

(C) The two position main landing gear modified to permit a three-degree increase in landing altitude when in position.

(D) Nose wheel spin-up required in order to reduce strut drag loads experienced during landing.

The engine access panels are clearly seen here in the open position. This maintenance procedure proved cumbersome and time consuming.
Courtesy National Naval Aviation Museum

415 is between tests and is further readied for others. This pre-production example appears fast just through simple inspection. *Courtesy U.S. Navy*

Carrier suitability tests would begin 23 July 1951 aboard the USS *Midway* (CVB-41) with LCDR Edward L. Feightner at the controls.

After 13 catapults and landings at the hand of Lt. Cdr. Edward L. Feightner, F7U-1 Bu No. 124415 suffered a structural failure behind the cockpit, briefly delaying trials. Unpredictable and inconsistent sink rates upon landing were blamed for this mishap. Deemed unfit for carrier use due to the obstructed pilot's view during landing brought about by the inordinately long nose gear oleo strut precipitated a total redesign of the F7U-1 airframe, eventually producing the F7U-3 variant. Testing would be terminated on 14 August 1951 predicated on the following Engineering Memo EM-1140:

> Engineering Memo 1140 is summarized in the following document: Summary Review of Corrective Actions Resulting From XF7U-1/F7U-1 Navy Evaluations and Their Relation to the F7U-3.
>
> Summary:
> This memorandum dated 28 May 1952 with enclosure presents a review of the deficiencies reported and action taken to correct them as a result of the several Navy evaluations of the XF7U-1 and F7U-1 airplanes. The chart in enclosure (1 located in Appendix A) also notes the F7U-3 position with regard to the reported deficiencies.

F7U-1 415 on the deck of the USS *Midway* (CVB-41), July 1951, being prepared for its carrier suitability tests. *Courtesy Author*

1. The first Navy evaluation of the XF7U-1 was made during November 1948 at Patuxent when Capt. F. M. Trapnell (now Read Admiral) made several flights in Bu No. 122472. His informal observations are reported in NATC, Patuxent River, Memorandum of Capt. F. M. Trapnell's Preliminary Evaluation of the XF7U-1, dated 16 November 1948, forwarded by Buder letter AER-DC-24, serial number 011230 of 15 December 1948.

2. The first formal Navy evaluation of the XF7U-1 took place during June, 1949, on airplane Bu No. 122474, five Navy pilots flew twenty-one flights, involving a total of fourteen flight hours. This evaluation was first reported by speed-letter, referencing NATC Patuxent River, Speed Letter to Buder reporting results of preliminary evaluation of XF7U-1, (9 June to 1 July 1949), XF7U-1 FT31-011, 13 July 1949, forwarded by Buder letter AER-AC-24, serial number 07292 of 3 August 1949 and then by final report NATC, Patuxent River final report on preliminary evaluation tests on model XF7U-1 airplane PTR-AC-214, FT31-030 of 21 November 1949.

As a result of this evaluation an extensive series of modifications was designed and incorporated in the XF7U-1 and subsequently in the F7U-2. These modifications included new fins and rudders, a yaw damper, and the redesigned feel system with the feel units in the wings. The wing speed brakes were modified at this time but no fuselage speed brakes were installed.

3. On 22 November 1949 Capt. Trapnell flew XF7U-1 BUNo. 122474 with the powered-control struts removed without encountering control sensitivity and thereby establishing that control sensitivity was not an inherent aerodynamic condition.

4. The next and actually final evaluation of the XF7U-1 took place at Ardmore, Oklahoma, in early March 1959. The tests involved seven flights, totaling eight flight hours by Lt. Col. M. E. Carl and Lc. Dr. J. R. Rees. This evaluation is reported in NATC, Patuxent River, memorandum report of Ardmore evaluation of XFU-1 (8 through 10 March 1950): XF7U-1 FT31-014 of 6 April 1950; forwarded to CVA by Bar, Dallas by No. A(s)8337/F1 serial number 0359 of 11 April 1950 the modifications outlined in paragraph 2 above corrected a substantial number of the earlier deficiencies but others were reported. With the loss of this the last XF7U-1 airplane on 7 July 1950, further corrections of deficiencies devolved on the F7U-1 airplanes.

5. Carrier suitability tests were conducted on F7U-1 airplane Bu No. 124415 between 24 June 1950 and 14 August 1951. On 7 July 1950, all F7U-1 aircraft were grounded as a result of the loss of F7U-1 Bu No. 124416 the aircraft were ungrounded on 21 August 1950 after a series of control system modifications had been incorporated and tested. NATC, Patuxent River, Service acceptance trials; carrier suitability tests, Project TL-D BIS-21133, F535-0157, reports on this phase of the F7U-1 evaluation. During the course of the trials a large number of discrepancies were corrected and consequently not reported in the "conclusion" to the subject report the enclosure of EM-1140 (in Appendix A) lists only the items reported as unacceptable or unsatisfactory or were recommendations are made that may be effective on the future F7U-3.

6. "NATC reports BIS-21133, FT31-0139 and FT31-024 are preliminary reports on the stability and control phase of the F7U-1 service acceptance service trials, and include only the lateral-directions tests performed to date. It is expected that upon the return of BUNo. 124419 to Patuxent and the completion of the contract demonstration by the contractor's pilot, additional tests will be conducted by NATC pilots.

Summary recommendations:

A. That modifications on remaining F7U-1 airframes be made to improve pilot's view of the carrier and landing approach.

B. To ascertain the effects of improved view on pilot's altitude and sinking speed.

C. To determine the minimum catapult speed with landing gear fully extended.

D. To develop techniques to aid the pilot in the determination of correct altitude adjustment on carrier approaches.

E. A new integral type hook be incorporated in lieu of existing latch.

F. A special ring retaining boot be incorporated in conjunction with use of tension ring-type hold back fitting.

G. A new bridle stop or catcher be developed.

H. To all existing F7U-1 aircraft to prevent nose gear cocking during flight.

I. To provide adequate clearance between the main landing gear doors and the swivel brake line fitting necessary to avoid jamming of gear during extension.

Note: in enclosure 1 EM 1140 Appendix A all 51 recommendations are cited. These existing recommendations are abbreviated at best.

A Program Chronological Record Summary of Tests
1. Test directive origination: 10 April 1950
2. Model F7U-1 Bu No. 124415 received: 24 June 1950
3. Instrumentation installation completed on aircraft 124415: 6 July 1950
4. Aircraft 124416 crashed killing its pilot: 6 July 1950
5. Grounding of all F7U-1 test vehicles: 7 July 1950
6. Tests resume: 24 August 1950
7. Shipboard tests begin: 23 July 1951
8. Carrier suitability tests terminated: 14 August 1951

Cutlass 415 just catapulted from the end of the carrier deck. The catapult cable can be viewed at the lower left of this picture and was quickly discarded for further use on future catapults. *Courtesy Author*

LCDR Edward L. Feightner flew Cutlass 415 on 13 catapults and recoveries. Here 415's arrestor hook is engaging the arrestor cable, bringing her to an abbreviated stop. *Courtesy Author*

415 on final approach with arrestor hook deployed. The Cutlass, by virtue of its elongated nose oleo strut, necessitates a rather nose high attitude during approach. *Courtesy Vought Heritage Center*

On a lighter note, two F7U-1s (Bu No. 124426 and No. 124427) were used in the Navy's Blue Angels aerial demonstration team circa 1952. Lt. Cdr. Feightner and lt. Harding C. MacKnight headed the flight team, responsible mainly for solo performances among their F9F-5 Panther brethren. One of "Whitey" Feightner's more memorable experiences would have to be the first public air show he flew in 1953. While in a full afterburner takeoff and steep climb his hydraulics went to zero. Anticipating a minimum altitude ejection he pulled the manual backup handle. Through the course of 10 seconds, which seemed like an eternity, the backup system became active, returning control back to Feightner just enough for him to make an emergency landing while trailing hydraulic fluid in a bright red flame. Upon landing the crowd went wild. What a performance! Encore!

Both 426 and 427 taking time out between performances for a photo op. *Courtesy Author*

F7U-1s Buno 12426 and 12427 were remanded to the Navy's Blue Angels Aerial Demonstration Team circa 1957. Here these center stage performers take time out for a photo op. *Courtesy Jay Miller Collection*

Their performances were short lived. The team only appeared in three engagements spanning from Philadelphia, PA, Columbus, OH, to Miami, FL. Due to a lack of spare parts both examples were relegated to maintenance training units. The other F7U-1s were flown by the advanced training command until they, too, conceded to a parts shortage as well. Some of the remaining unflyable examples were sent to the Naval Air Technical Training Command at Memphis, TN, and utilized as maintenance trainers. Experience acquired at this juncture in testing provided valuable data for the developmental program to continue.

The United States Air Force demonstrated keen interest in the F7U-1 when contacted by Vought. Air Force Technical Report No. AFFTC-52-13, dated 17 March 1952, "Flight Test Evaluation of a Chance Vought F7U-1 Airplane," by Messrs. Fred J. Ascani and Frank K. Everest, states the following:

It is concluded that:
a) The longitudinal trim change evidenced as a tendency to pitch nose down, which is encountered at .91 indicated mach number, is unacceptable for a fighter-bomber type airplane.
b) The lateral-directional dynamic stability is not entirely satisfactory for a gun platform, even with presently installed damping device operating.
c) Longitudinal control is restricted or limited by the high stick force per "G" gradient and by the decrease in elevon power or increased instability encountered at high mach number.
d) Manual operation of the slats requires an added operation which could be avoided if the slat operation were automatic.

In spite of the negative tone overseeing these conclusions overall attitude remained favorable. Nevertheless, the Air Force declined any further interest in the Cutlass.

This model of either 426 or 427 is an excellent representation of the actual aircraft. *Courtesy Author*

Both performers taking time between or before an airshow, which actually only spanned three: one in Philadelphia, PA.; Columbus, OH; and Miami, Fl. Due to parts shortages these examples were eventually remanded to maintenance training units. Because of their high speed and phenomenal roll rate (540°/sec) they were the highlight of the show. *Courtesy Vought Heritage Foundation*

77

Chapter 6

Further Development of the Cutlass

It became blatantly apparent early on in the initial flight test program of the F7U-1 that it possessed some fundamental shortcomings. This problem was temporarily remedied with Vought's V-366 interim proposal through a preliminary contract detailed specification Navawe SD-430-2, dated 9 May 1949, which insured an order for 88 examples of the F7U-2 Cutlass that were assigned Bu Nos. 125322 thru 125411. The amended proposal letter E-3127, dated 9 December 1949, specified the following:

Table 6-1

Description	Fighter (normal weight)	Fighter (max weight)
Gross weight (lbs) (not guaranteed)	21,505	25,105
Fuel Quantity Gallons	971	1,471
Max Speed	537KT (618 Mph)	
Stalling Speed w/o Power	104.5KT (120 Mph)	
Rate of Climb at Takeoff	850FPM	1,080FPM
Service Ceiling @ military thrust Full Load in FT	41,000FT	

Engine Specification Westinghouse J34-WE-32 Turbojet

Other more salient design aspects would include improved speed brakes and directional controls. A drooped or variable position nose accompanied by an elevated pilot seat was introduced by Vought engineers to improve the pilot's visibility upon landing and take off. These design highlights were included in the initial contract, and in turn red penciled and amended, confirming a "Final Draft" outlined in letter E-3127, only to be cancelled on 8 December 1949 in favor of Vought's latest rendition, the F7U-3. All subsequent man hours were transferred to the new airframe and the preparation of Vought's newest proposal.

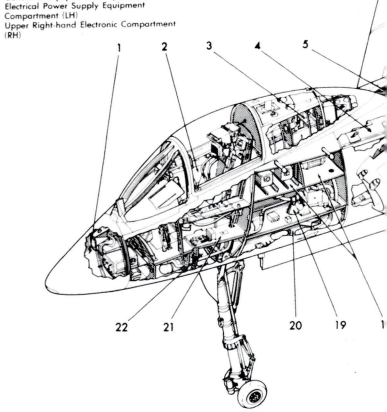

1. Radome Compartment
2. Cockpit Compartment
3. Aft Canopy Compartment
4. Forward Fuselage Fuel Cell Compartment
5. Mid Fuselage Fuel Cell Compartment
6. Ammunition Compartment (RH and LH)
7. Utility Hydraulic Reservoir Compartment
8. Fuselage Aft Fuel Cell Compartment
9. Afterburner Compartment
10. Yaw Damper Servo Compartment (RH and LH)
11. Main Gear Wheel Well Compartment (RH and LH)
12. Power Control Cylinder Compartment (RH and LH)
13. Aft Center Section Fuel Cell Compartment (RH and LH)
14. Forward Center Section Fuel Cell Compartment (RH and LH)
15. Engine Compartment (RH and LH)
16. Gun Bay Compartment (RH and LH)
17. Generator Equipment Compartment
18. Electrical Power Supply Equipment Compartment (LH) Upper Right-hand Electronic Compartment (RH)
19. Air-conditioning Compartment (LH) Lower Right-hand Electronic Compartment (RH)
20. Nose Gear Wheel Well Compartment
21. Console Compartment (RH and LH)
22. Subcockpit Electronic Compartment
23. Outer Panel Fuel Cells (F7U-3M and 3P only)

Cutaways are extremely useful in orientating the reader to the general component breakdown of the aircraft in question. This Cutlass illustration highlights this quite nicely. *Courtesy Author*

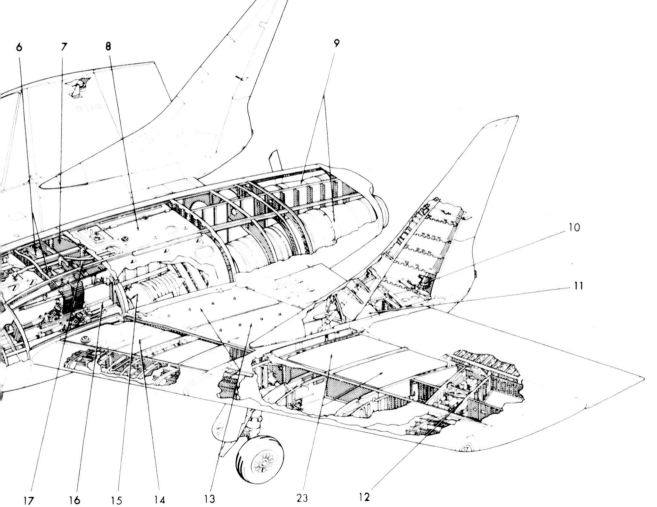

79

Detailed specification SD-430-3 of the F7U-3 model aircraft, dated 28 March 1950, specified the following in paragraph 1b, "The airplane shall take off from the decks of the CV-34 and the CVB-41 class carrier with the aid of the H8-H4-1 catapults, respectively with the useful lead specified....The airplane shall land on the decks of the CV-34 and the CVB-41 class carriers in the Mark 5 arresting gear, and on an ordinary landing field."

Further stipulated in paragraph 102a under "Characteristics" were the following:

Table 6-2

Description
weight (in lbs)
A Fighter (1380 gallons of fuel)
28,244
B Fighter (with 2.75" rockets and 1380 gallons of fuel)
29,454
C Fighter-Bomber (with 4000# bombs and
1495 gallons of fuel)
31,395

Table 6-3

Engine specified: Westinghouse J46-WE-2 Turbojet
Performance data is as follows:
High speed level flight as sea-level maximum thrust
combat load in KTS
614 (706 Mph)
Stalling Speed w/o power, gross weight 60%
of total fuel (knots)
101 (116 Mph)
Rate of climb, sea-level max thrust combat load (FPM)
18,510
Rate of climb at sea-level military thrust
combat load (FPM)
6,240
Combat radius at full load (knots)
500 (576 Mph)
Combat radius (30% boost) starting with full
load (knots)
530 (610 Mph)

Under contract NOa (5) 51-156, 28 airframes of the F7U-3 were being developed with the expressed intent to be powered by the Westinghouse J46-WE-2 turbojets. Due to developmental problems coinciding with the Westinghouse unit, Allison J35-A-29 engines were substituted in order to facilitate flight testing.

As time would provide, the Westinghouse J46-WE-2 engine units were reverted to airframes 17 through 28. This engine was again specified in SD-430-3-1 and issued 29 January 1952. Within the course of 23 months, between the initialization of the original contract for 212 airframes, a multitude of changes embraced the final design architecture involving the F7U-3.

These changes are reflected in MCRs No 1, 2, 6, 9, 10, 13, 14, 15, 18, and 22. Interim modifications of the F7U-3 are reflected in MCRs 4 and 5, accompanied by an effort to reduce

airframe weight and improve pilot visibility in MCR No 8. In its zeal for overall improvement, Vought nefariously allowed this once trim fighter to nearly double in weight. This is evident in the following chart:

Table 6-4

Aircraft	With fuel loaded in lbs	Without fuel loaded in lbs
XF7U-1	14,655	10,238
F7U-1	18,195	13,770
(Proposed) F7U-2	21,505	14,135
F7U-3	28,244	17,770

It can be readily determined upon simple inspection that the F7U-3 almost doubled in weight, or 92.7%, with an overall fuel load increase from 2.21 tons to 5.23 tons (236.6%).

Conscious of this fact, a total sum of 729 pounds were eliminated from the overall design. Hindsight would reveal this drastic and robust increase in weight could be attributed to all the structural and equipment upgrades incorporated in the latest design configuration. As further changes took place so did its gain in weight. Estimates of gross weights are as follows:

Table 6-5

Description	With fuel load in lbs	W/o fuel load in lbs
Fighter (1320 gallons of fuel)	27,060	17,041
Fighter with 2.75" rockets (1320 gallons of fuel)	28,010	17,991
Fighter Bomber (2-2000# bombs) (1320 gallons of fuel)	31,310	21,291

Performance
High speed, in level flight, in military thrust,
full combat load, not less than
567 KTS (652 Mph)
Stalling speed at sea-level without power,
full load, not greater than
114KTS (131 Mph)
Rate of climb at takeoff, Maximum thrust,
95°F day, at 115KTS
2,250 FPM
Service ceiling, normal thrust, combat load,
not less than
40,300ft

F7U-3 Design
Chance Vought predicated its F7U-3 design upon the sequestered and incremental improvements of the F7U- type. In many respects, though, this new variant underwent a total redesign, and bore limited semblance to the former. The emphasis placed upon the accommodation of new and advanced equipment placed special attention on the producibility of the new design.

The F7U-3 assembly lines were bursting with activity at Vought's Dallas, Texas, plant. One hundred eighty examples were eventually produced, culminating in 307 examples of all variants produced. *Courtesy Tom Cathcart*

The dash three Cutlass was actually easier to manufacture than its F7U-1 counterparts due to the adherence to the companies' master plan. *Courtesy Tom Cathcart*

The end of the line. Cutlass production is halted due to Vought's newest thoroughbred, the F8U-1 Crusader. Note the Crusader in the foreground. *Courtesy Vought Heritage Foundation*

F7U-3s stored outside Vought's manufacturing facility in Dallas, Texas, awaiting their Westinghouse J46-WE-8A turbojets. *Courtesy Vought Hertiage Foundation*

Over 100 new access panels were added to the F7U-3's airframe and are evident in this photo. The starboard electronics bay access panel is opened, demonstrating this facet in the new design. *Courtesy Author*

Certain manufacturing problems experienced in the F7U-1 program were addressed through extensive redesign, which later yielded "cleaner" design features, thus increasing the ease of fabrication. Design inroads were achieved at all connection points by placing all electrical lines on the right and all hydraulic lines on the left side of the fuselage to coincide with the major subassembly juncture points. Vought engineers, through their tireless efforts, established over 100 new structural access points, accentuating its ease of assembly and field maintenance on the deck or runway. Particular attention addressing the pilot's field of vision, or lack of, initiated a total cockpit redesign.

Final answer as to the details of the F7U-3 master plan developed for such circumstances would be able to accommodate these ongoing changes when experienced.

The Master Plan, Blue Book
The master plan, in essence, is the combined effort, a product of collusion between the management, engineering department, materials department, and the manufacturing department. No one person is singularly responsible for the orchestration and execution of scheduling and the final design related to the F7U-3. The master plan's primary function was to provide the orderly control of the F7U-3 programs from engineer's slide rule to actual flight. This master plan would attain its interim goals through the introduction of recorded truths that were recognized by management as a "prerequisite to the successful production and delivery of the airplane" outlined in the company's bible, "The Blue Book."

Instituted at this critical juncture in the company's history, while fundamentally facing three challenges in the F7U-3 program, the company documented their goals as being:

1. "To deliver an end product which, when compared to their competitors' airplanes, will be better. Grumman is building the F 10-F. It is designed for approximately the same performance as the F7U-3. It is timed to be in a flight evaluation about the same time as the F7U-3. In all probability, for the long pull, the navy will place continuing orders from only one of the two types, the better of the two. It will be Grumman or Chance Vought".
2. "To deliver the F7U-3 in less time than Vought has produced a new model in years. Our plane must be completed and ready for the competition at approximately the same time as Grumman's model. This means the first F7U-3 must be ready for acceptance in December, 1951.
3. "To deliver the F7U-3 at a lower cost than Vought has been building airplanes. Our airplanes must be at least in line with the competition, in so far as costs are concerned. It will require a superior of managing for Vought to do the F7U-3 job in time, at the cost, and with the product performance required. In order to do a good job of managing, we must first do a good job of planning. Development of the master plans for the F7U-3 is primarily the job of relatively few people in Vought's management organization. The managing of the master plan for this airplane becomes a responsibility for every member of the management team. In the purpose of the F7U-3 Blue Book, therefore, is to outline the broad plans for this job: define basic responsibilities, set forth the cost standards we must meet, explain the controls we have set for ourselves, and establish the time table for this entire operation."

Time Table- F7U-3 Master Plan

Due Date
mock up complete
March 31, 1950
First drawings released by engineering department
April, 1950
Complete release of engineering design
Dec. 8, 1950
Start of tool fabrication
June 1, 1950
Completion of all tooling necessary to produce first airplane

Detail tools
April 30, 1951
Subassembly tools
June 1, 1951
Major assembly fixtures
June 1, 1951
Initial release of manufacturing work orders
Nov. 13, 1950
Start of detail fabrication
Nov. 28, 1950

First Production Airplane	Static Test Article Assembly Operations
Center Section wing	
Start leading edge and beam assembly March 14, 1951	Feb. 15, 1951
Start loading major C.S jig April 4, 1951	March 8, 1951
Center section structure complete May 15, 1951	April 18, 1951
Center section Installation complete June 6, 1951	May 9, 1951
Front Section Fuselage	
Start loading major F.S jig April 11, 1951	March 15, 1951
Front section structure complete June 6, 1951	May 9, 1951
Front section structure complete July 19, 1951	June 21, 1951
Aft Section Fuselage	
Start loading major A.S jig June 21, 1951	May 24, 1951
Aft section structure complete July 19, 1951	June 21, 1951
Outer Panel Wing	
Start leading edge and beam assembly May 31, 1951	May 3, 1951
Start loading major O.P. jig June 21, 1951	May 24, 1951
Outer panel structure complete July 19, 1951	June 21, 1951
Outer panel installations complete Aug. 23, 1951	July 13, 1951
Engines	
Start assembly of engines Aug. 20, 1951	
Engine assembly complete Sept. 7, 1951	
Engine test stand operations complete Sept. 14, 1951	
Final Assembly at Airport	
Start joining major sections July 20, 1951	June 22, 1951
Airplane shop complete Sept. 28, 1951	June 27, 1951
Initial Flight November 1951	
Navy Acceptance Dec. 31, 1951	

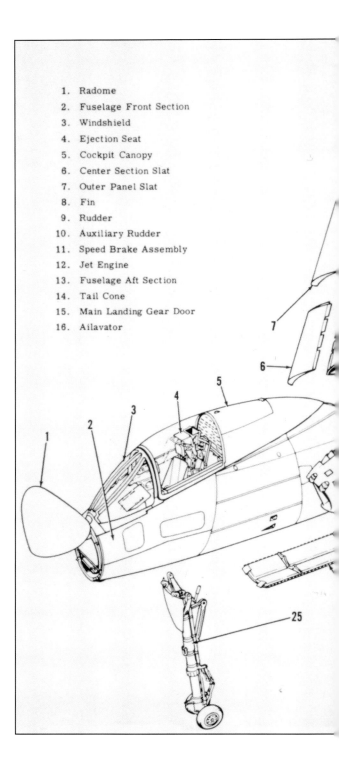

1. Radome
2. Fuselage Front Section
3. Windshield
4. Ejection Seat
5. Cockpit Canopy
6. Center Section Slat
7. Outer Panel Slat
8. Fin
9. Rudder
10. Auxiliary Rudder
11. Speed Brake Assembly
12. Jet Engine
13. Fuselage Aft Section
14. Tail Cone
15. Main Landing Gear Door
16. Ailavator

In reality, the first flight took place on 12 December 1951 from Dallas, with the company pilot, John McGuyrt, at the controls. Soon after, the Navy accepted the Cutlass with a Bu No. 128454 for initial test and evaluation.

F7U-3 Buno 128454, first flown on 12 December 1951 by Vought test pilot John McGuyrt, is captured in flight high over Dallas, Texas. *Courtesy Author*

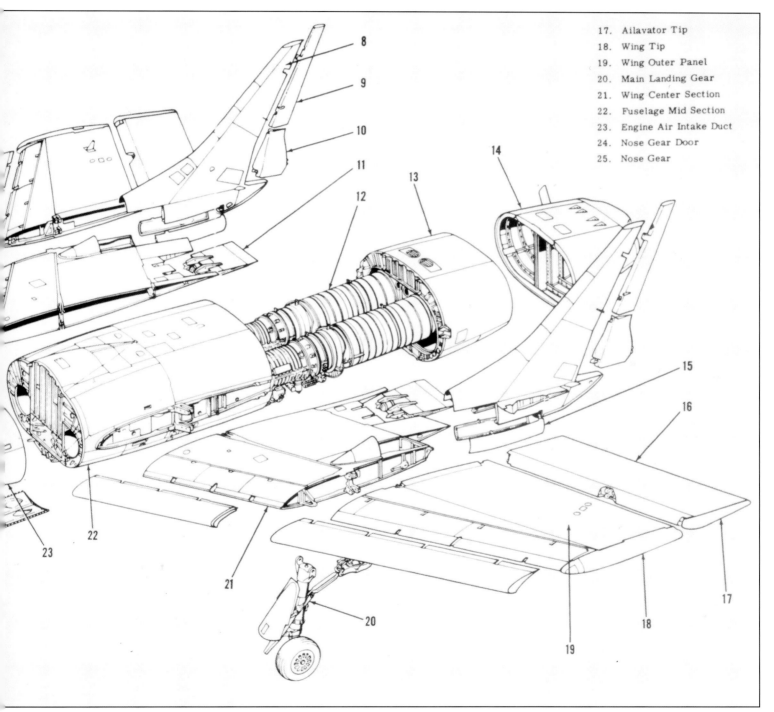

17. Ailavator Tip
18. Wing Tip
19. Wing Outer Panel
20. Main Landing Gear
21. Wing Center Section
22. Fuselage Mid Section
23. Engine Air Intake Duct
24. Nose Gear Door
25. Nose Gear

This photo denotes an entire component breakdown of the F7U-3 based on the master plan, blue book prioritized assembly architecture. *Courtesy Author*

In relation to the Blue Book, it specifically outlined and prioritized the development of the subassembly and established a hierarchy of development to coincide with the advanced scheduling once set forth. They are:

AA Priority
Main loading gear and nose gear
Center section main beam forging
A Priority
Other major forgings, such as wing fittings
Center section wing structure
Midsection fuselage structure
Fuselage nose cone (Radome)
B Priority
Front section fuselage structure
Cockpit, windshield, and canopy
Fins and rudders
Center sections slats
C Priority
Aft section fuselage structure
Outer panel wing structure
Outer panel slats
Speed brakes
Ailevators

The more ambient design aspects of the F7U-3 will be discussed in terms of the hierarchy of prioritization

F7U-3 Buno 128451 is the number one dash 3 Cutlass produced without the advent of newly acquired flight test data from the XF7U-1 and F7U-1. Notable similarities to that of the dash one lie in the canopy design, single nose wheel, and a more rounded radome. Hence, it was referred to as the bulb nose Cutlass and retained this characterization for the first 16 production examples out of the initial production batch of 28 aircraft. *Courtesy Bill Spidel*

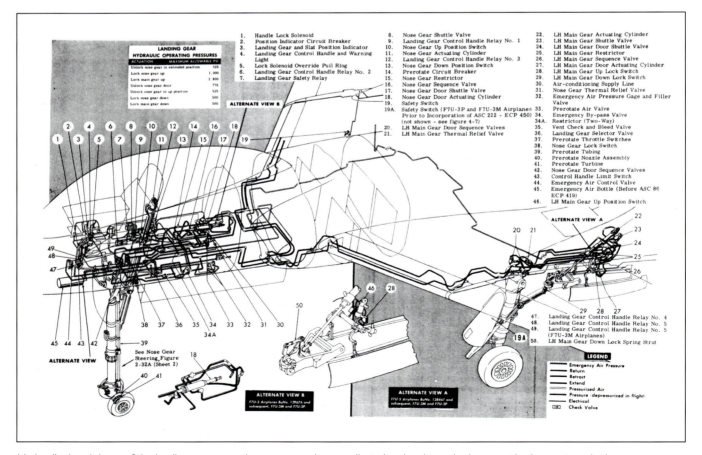

Hydraulics breakdown of the landing gear operation appears quite complicated and embraced subsequent backup systems in the event of a major system malfunction. *Courtesy Author*

AA Priority

This priority involves the main landing gear, nose gear, and center section main beam forging. Because of the certain acquisition of more airframe weight, Vought engineers focused their attention on strengthening the main and nose gear auto struts, as well as a hold back arrangement to aid in catapulting. The first 16 production F7U-3s were built without the benefit of data directly acquired from the XF7U-1 and F7U-1 evaluations. Subsequently, the nose gear consisted of one steerable wheel without the aid of additional strengthening. This oversight was eventually corrected in example airframe 17 onwards with the incorporation of a dual steerable nose wheel/oleo strut arrangement, vastly improving overall strength and functionality. The final extension of the nose gear oleo strut would provide a 20° overall angle of incidence while retaining its original pre-rotation feature. This further enhanced the airfcraft's lift/drag ratio, which was needed in lieu of its massive weight gain. The main wheels and oleo struts were redesigned disregarding its original two part positioning and included a holdback mechanism, ensuring the aircraft's proper angle of incidence during the catapult operation.

The center section main beam forging refers to the center section wing main structural beam forging and, due to its respective design, afforded a cleaner fabrication of the article, enhancing ease of manufacturing. The beam is substantially more robust in appearance, implying greater strength in its overall design architecture.

A Priority

The other forgings would preclude and include wing fittings at this stage in priority, recognizing greater strength and adaptability in the fabrication process.

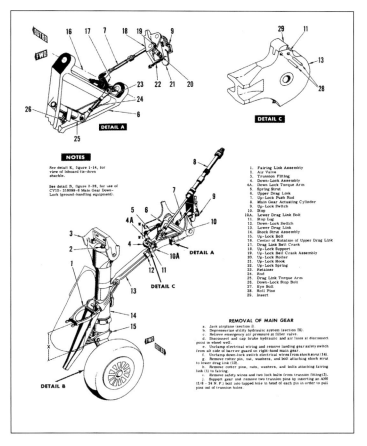

Main landing gear illustrated in this photo reveals the stout resilience of its design, implying strength. *Courtesy Author*

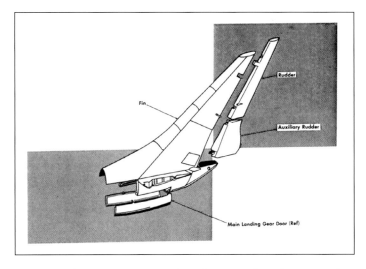

The vertical fin, especially the dorsal portion, was enlarged to accomodate equipment as well as aerodynamic changes to the overall airframe. *Courtesy Author*

The center section wing structure was significantly redesigned "structurally" to include ample amounts of access panels and the enlargement of the entire wing structure to 39 feet 8 inches and a 38° sweep angle. The center section, including the outer wing panels, boasts a robust 535.5 square feet and is stressed to +7G to -9G, respectively. Again, this segment in the overall structure integration of the airframe is significant in importance because it embodies and positions the vertical fins and the main landing gear responsible for the absorption of flight loads upon landing. Careful attention was also directed in the location of fuel cells, integrated structurally and as external additions to the airframe overall.

The midsection fuselage structure involves the air intakes, 20mm gun emplacements, and center wing attachment points. The air intakes were extended a full two feet beyond the leading edge of the wing and enlarged to accommodate the increase in airflow for the new Westinghouse J46-WE-2 turbojets. The center fuselage section also includes the air/engine intake ducting, which is responsible for airframe/engine cooling as well. This system is responsible for the decrease in sonic and transonic airflow to that of subsonic flow for proper engine aspiration to take place.

Wing attachment forgings are responsible for the permanent attachment of the wings to the fuselage center section. Flight loads are reacted through these forgings and through the fuselage in order to ensure safe and proficient management of such loading conditions.

This unfinished center section structure conveys the brute strength this assembly possessed in its overall contribution to this aircraft's structural integrity. *Courtesy Vought Heritage foundation*

Internal framework is exposed here behind the fuselage break at station 256. Green paint is essentially zinc chromate primer used as a corrosion retardant to great effect. Notice how the bulkheads are integrated, interlocked to provide great strength at low weight. *Courtesy Tom Cathcart*

All four 20mm gun emplacements were located in pairs above each air intake. Gun gas discharge during firing was later found to be ingested by the engines, resulting in compressor stalls and flameouts. Eventually stainless steel louvers were added above each emplacement, venting the discharge directly into the air and thus avoiding any further trouble. Each gun, equipped with 720 rounds of ammunition, was eventually guided by a MK.8 gun sight and APC-30 ranging radar.

The radome was constructed primarily of fabrilited houses (for the F7U-3), the APC-30 ranging radar, and the APQ-51 dish antenna (for the F7U-3M). It supports the angle of yaw relative wind transducer. Cooling would be achieved through air exhausting from the cockpit area.

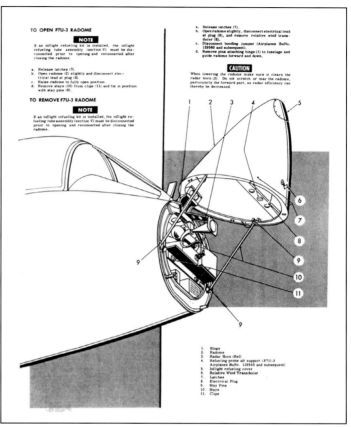

Target acquisition and gun aiming were encompassed by the APC-30 ranging radar. Component breakdown is shown and was functionally quite simple. *Courtesy Author*

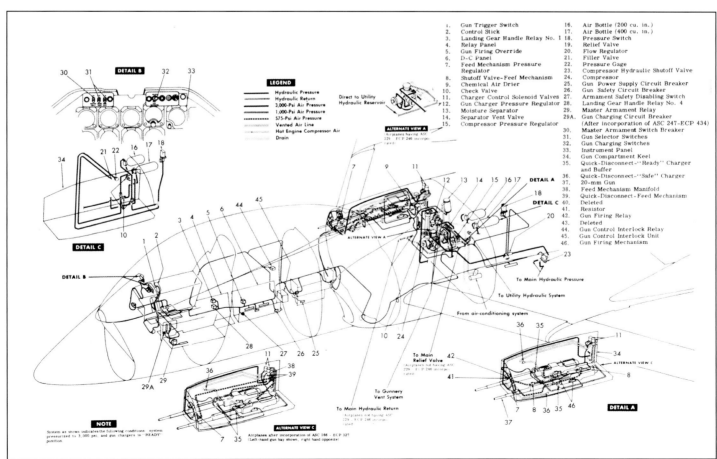

Gun emplacement provided ease of maintenance and accessibility. Assembled in modules, quick changes were thus made possible. *Courtesy Author*

B Priority

The front section fuselage structure would include the cockpit, radome, nose gear wheel well, and canopy. The entire fuselage would be enlarged to dimensions 43 feet and 1 inch. The cockpit, a major source of continuous frustration for Vought engineers, found solace in the complete redesign, including a two position pilot's seat (for enhancing visibility), a smaller radome, and a hunched canopy, enabling the latter to take place. This was not the case in the first 16 production examples utilizing the adjustable pilot seat, with no apparent reduction in the size of the radome or increased size of the canopy. The first 16 examples were referred to as the Bulb Nose Cutlass and were modified to more exacting design standards implemented on the 17th example and onwards.

F7U-3 Buno 128452, the second produced in the initial production batch of 28 airframes, was the second of the first 16 produced, coining the name Bulb Nose due to the retention of some F7U-1 features. *Courtesy Author*

F7U-3 Buno 128461, the tenth of the first 16 produced Bulb Nose Cutlass, was remanded to the Naval Test Center in 1954. *Courtesy Author*

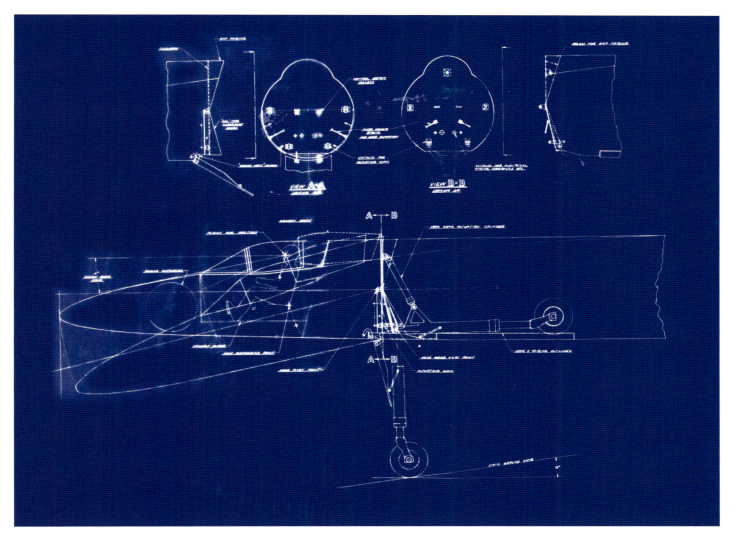

Vought engineers tried in vane to correct visual difficulties experienced by all pilots while flying the Cutlass. Although novel and pragmatic in many ways, this design was eventually discarded due to insufficient aerodynamic data. *Courtesy Vought Heritage Fundation*

During this vetting process, to resolve the pilot's landing visibility difficulties an evaluation of a tilting cockpit design was initiated on 29 May 1952 and involved the following engineering memo, EM-894:

1. Summary

A study was made to determine the weight increase resulting from the installation of a tilting cockpit and nose section. The tilting cockpit (as configured in CVS-35431) provided additional vision over the nose equal in angle to the amount of tilt, and would increase the airplane weight by 163 pounds (not including a size factor).

I. Weight Analysis

In this study, the F7U-3 was used as a source of data, and the following values were considered reasonable:

1. Weight of nose section, FWD. of pivot point- 2,500 lb
2. Landing accelerations-6.55g up and 4.45g aft: 1.17g side (limit)
3. Flight loading conditions
a. 7.5g symmetrical pull out (limit)
b. 6.0g rolling pull out with 220lb/ft^2 side air load (limit)

Loads based on the above data were used to approximate the physical size of the tilting mechanism, and thus estimate the resulting weight. Weight increases in basic structures, hydraulics, electrical installations, and controls were obtained by con group con.

The weight breakdown based on use of the nose gear actuation cylinder for cockpit tilting is as follows:

 Description
Pounds
 1. Pivot fittings, pins, links, and hardware
 20
 2. Side clearance doors, actuating rods, and bracket installations

3. Additional bulkhead for nose section   42
4. Additional weight of structure for load
    distributions   49
5. Increase in nose gear actuation cylinder
    assuming the cylinder is not oversized to the
    point of being able to assimilate a retraction
    load of 2,800 lbs   10
6. Sheet metal of nose section and fuselage   5
7. Increase in electrical lines   5
8. Increase in hydraulic lines   4
9. Increase in mechanical controls   5
10. Increase in air-conditioning   2
total   148
contingency (10%)   163

Note that the attempt to eliminate the canopy problems associated with pivoting the nose at the seat bulkhead results in the pivot, and hence the nose gear, being moved aft of the seat bulkhead: This introduced an inherent weight penalty equal to a portion of the new bulkhead weight. This may be offset to some extent by the shorter nose gear, but a net penalty of as much as 30 pounds could probably exist which would be in addition to the above weight.

II. Operation of Tilting Mechanism (see enclosure CVS 35431)

The nose section rotates about two pivot points located on the fuselage bulkhead. Movement is affected by the actuating lines which tie into lugs on the nose gear strut. The nose gear actuation cylinder, acting through the nose gear strut, is the source of motive power.

During the extension of the nose gear and the lowering of the nose, the opening of the nose gear strut fairing accounts for 1/3 of the lower joint overlap. The other 2/3 of the overlap is provided by 2 inch gill type doors which are strut connected to the fuselage. The lowering of the nose causes the two side doors to open. The gap above the pivot point is covered by a sheet metal fairing when the nose is down.

III. Typical Configuration for Nose Tilt of 14°

Flight Condition Down Vision Over Center Line of Nose	Angle of Attack Angle of Cockpit 0° Incidence Floor to Horizon
Cruise	0°
-11°(no tilt)	0°
Approach (min speed)	+20°
-5°(tilted)	+6°
Static on Ground	+8°
-17°(tilted)	-6°

IV. Conclusions
A. Advantages of tilting nose
1. Solves the vision problem
2. Pilots seated attitude is normal during final approach
3. Mechanism is a direct mechanical linkage to nose gear
4. Possible future development of nose section into ejectional pop

B. Disadvantages of Tilting Nose
1. Additional weight of 163 lbs without size factor
2. Possible aerodynamic problems during final approach
3. Another gadget to "complicate" maintenance

Expert opinion from retired Vought personnel once involved in the Cutlass program would allude to the fact that not enough aerodynamic data became available in the evaluation of this major design change.

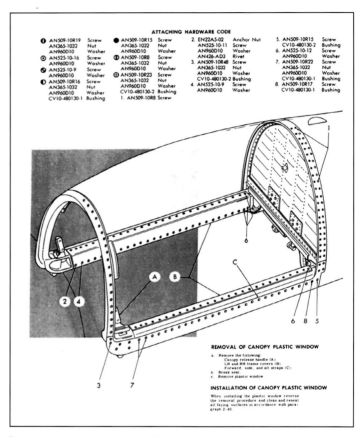

Redesigning the canopy with this pronounced hunch enabled pilots to reset their two position Vought ejection seat, thus enhancing the visibility of the pilots upon landing. Although a big improvement, it failed to negate this problem entirely. *Courtesy Author*

With that in mind, great strides were enacted on behalf of engineers not to contribute to the overly complicated design already being pursued.

The accepted solution found credence in retaining the pilot's two position seat, reducing the radome's overall stature, and adding a pronounced hunch in the canopy, which allowed the degree of freedom required for proper adjustment of the pilot's seat to occur.

The cockpit tub, overall enlarged from its predecessor on the F7U-1, afforded generous amounts of space occupying Vought's company built 2 position ejection seat, control yoke employing artificial feel from its newly redesigned hydraulic flight control system. Lessons learned—"hard lessons" from XF7U-1 and F7U-1 flight testing—motivated Vought to redesign its hydraulically controlled flight, incorporating artificial feel in the system architecture. Hydraulic pressure for ailevator control was now supplied through two sources, which are identified as power control systems Number 1 and Number 2. The two systems, Number 1 being the larger function concurrently, provided pressure from two separate pumps located on each turbojet. If for any reason the engines failed or were impeded in any manner, by virtue of windmilling the engines in free stream air occurring around 200 knots still provided the power to maintain successful operations of the pumps to facilitate aerodynamic control of the aircraft. Below 200 knots, a specially designed electric pump provided necessary hydraulic pressure for only 3 minutes.

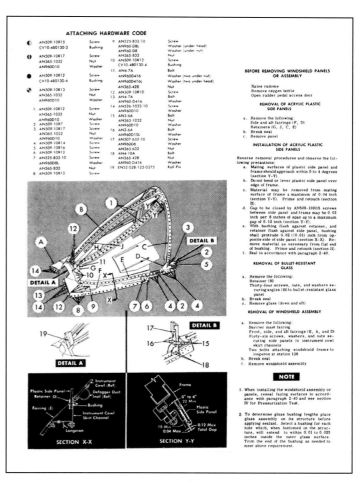

The cockpit wind screen is solely fabricated from acrylic plastic reinforced by an aluminum frame. *Courtesy Author*

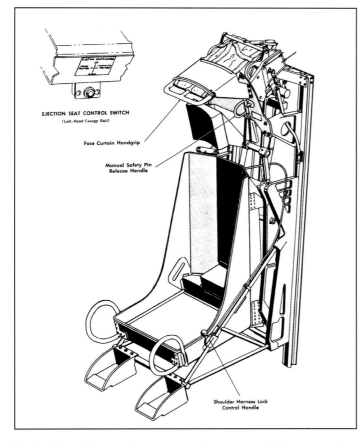

Vought's 2 position ejection seat was well used, especially by novice pilots vastly unfamiliar with the whims and peculiarities that the Cutlass was known to have. *Courtesy Author*

The cockpit front wind screen is solely fabricated from plastic (acrylic), maintaining an all aluminum mounting frame, and houses the MK.8 gun sight.

The F7U-3 design still retains the twin vertical stabilizers, maintaining the original height embraced by it predecessors with one exception. The dorsal portions of the stabilizer fin fillets were increased in size in order to accommodate the structural upgrades deemed necessary in this latest design. With the fins structurally enhanced, the attachment of the main rudder accompanied by an auxiliary rudder is accomplished. The lower fin stub houses the improved main landing gear. Hand holds and foot steps were also included in the initial design phase of the fin, further improving accessibility to maintenance points on the airframe.

Center section slats are retained from previous designs and operate in unison with the outer panel slats, providing additional lift and boundary layer control over the upper portion of the entire wing. Through this process additional lift can be obtained at much slower air speeds, providing the much needed handling characteristics required during takeoff and landing. During this critical phase of landing both the leading edge slats and the main landing gear are interlocked and fully deployed. Upon landing the slats would then be returned to their former position through manual retraction.

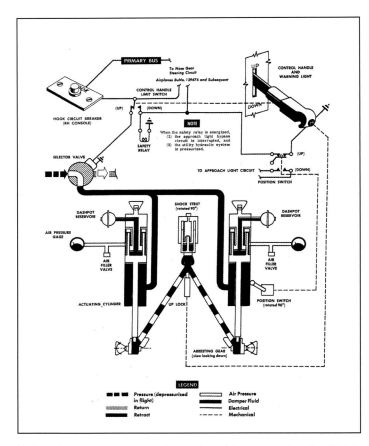

V shaped arrester gear was used over that of the one used on the F7U-1. It was functionally stronger than the former through its inherent V shaped design, and also through its attachment points located on the lower aft fuselage. *Courtesy Author*

Subsystems and Power Plant

Several important subsystems immediately stand out and provide the needed functionality unique to that of the Cutlass. These would be the cockpit pressurization and air-conditioning, the ailevator control and feel system, and flight stabilization system. The Cutlass also utilized Westinghouse's newest turbojet contender, the J46-WE-8A, with factory built afterburners.

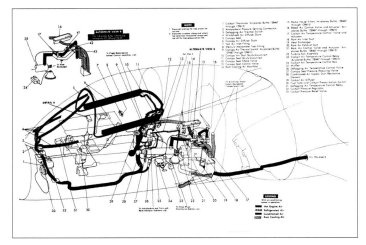

Cockpit air conditioning, vital in keeping all electronic equipment cool and operating well within temperature limits, proved to be rather complex and at times challenging in maintaining the Cutlass. *Courtesy Author*

C Priority: Aft Fuselage

The aft fuselage assembly is comprised of significant amounts of 18-8 stainless steel and is responsible for the retention of the aft portion of the turbojets and their subsequent afterburners. Also included are the rear center section wing panel attachments points as well as the speed brakes. The newly designed arrestor gear is also positioned in this area and sports a V-shaped arm, later providing exceptional performance in arrested carrier landings.

The outer panel wing structure involves that portion of the wing extending beyond the vertical stabilizer and wing folding juncture. This included the outer lading edge slat, which is also activated hydraulically. Outer wing beam forgings were designed in conjunction to that of their center section cousins and fabricated to the same exacting standards.

Speed brakes were two clam shell units initialized hydraulically and located on the trailing edge of the wing, positioned inwardly between the aft fuselage section and the vertical stabilizer (fin). These were moderately enlarged to provide additional speed control whether in the air or on the deck, which proved to be a design and developmental ally as a whole.

Engine compressor air is used primarily in the heating, cooling, and overall ventilation, including fog removal and the pressurization of the cockpit. Cockpit air conditioning manifests itself by the inclusion of hot compressor bleed air primarily divided into two streams: the first stream flows through the air cycle refrigeration unit while the other stream takes a deferred path around the unit. Both streams unite in a chamber behind the unit and are ducted into the cockpit. Included are three points of entry, which are comprised of the cockpit air diffuser that is mounted off center behind the ejection seat, the windshield air diffuser ducts, and lastly the canopy air diffuser ducts. The stream that is routed through the refrigeration unit is cooled by heat transferred via thermodynamic expansion to a low temperature. Temperature control is achieved through the self modulating qualities of each stream expressed during the re-unification process in the chamber prior to cockpit entry. On a broader note, cabin temperature is monitored by a device better known as a thermistor, and is activated if the temperature limits are exceeded. It accomplishes its task of monitoring temperature extremes by initiating an electrical imbalance across a bridge circuit, activating a current direction sensitive micropositioner relay. A "hot" or "cold" relay is then activated, redirecting the cockpit air temperature within safe limits. Temperature control is maintained either by manual or automatic means.

Cockpit Pressurization

Cockpit pressurization is predicated on normal or combat schedules. Both are identical up to and including 35,000 feet. Normal pressurizations maintain a 3.3 psi pressure differential from 35,000 feet to maximum altitude. Combat pressurization pressure, or the difference in this case, decreases from 35,000 feet and is reduced to a mere 1.3 psi at 47,000 feet. Combat differential pressure is maintained above 47,000 feet if necessary, and is low enough to prevent physical injury of the pilot in the event that explosive decompression of the cockpit should occur. If for some unexplainable reason over-pressurization should occur a cabin relief valve activates, thus alleviating any structural damage to the airplane. This valve also opened, preventing pressure from dropping below -0.25 psi during vertical dives.

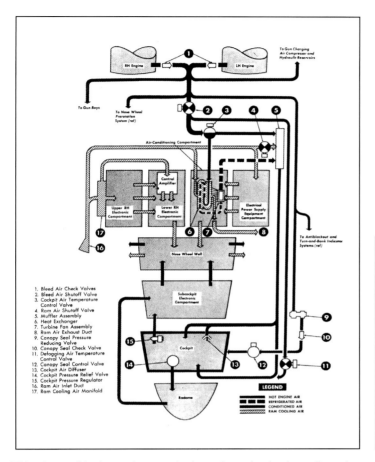

This air conditioning and pressurization schematic clearly outlines the component hierarchy involved in these systems. *Courtesy Author*

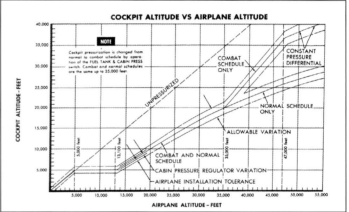

Cockpit pressurization schedule is predicated upon cockpit altitude (internal cockpit pressure) versus airplane altitude (outside pressure). *Courtesy Author*

Ailevator Control and Feel System

The principal, or most identifying characteristic of the Cutlass lies in and is accentuated by its twin vertical tails. These vertical stabilizers, as already ascertained, provide the directional control for the airplane. Pitch and roll control is provided by a device known as an ailevator. This device provides the combined usage of ailerons and elevators and is operated by an irreversible hydraulic system. Pilot inputs to the control yoke govern the variable positioning of the ailevators during flight. When an irreversible hydraulic system is used no aerodynamic forces are felt at the control stick, so in order for the pilot not to overfly or inadvertently overstress the airframe an artificial feel system was introduced to simulate these forces.

During normal operating conditions the ailevators are controlled by the pilot's inputs into the control yoke. Their differential usage as ailerons and elevators is accomplished through mixing linkage transmitted through each wing by means of control rods, bell cranks, idlers, and walking beams. This mixed linkage terminates at two slider valves located in tandem on each hydraulic ailevator actuating cylinder. Each slider valve is responsible for regulating the hydraulic flow emanating from both hydraulic systems, initiating the extension or retraction of the pistons and thus raising or lowering the ailevators.

Attached to each slider valve would be a structural feedback rod assembly, and is further positioned on the outer panel wing structure near the ailevator hinge line. Its sole function is to improve or enhance the operation of the slider valve brought about through structural deflections when in operation. A valve force reduction strut is also attached to the entire assembly which affords added stability.

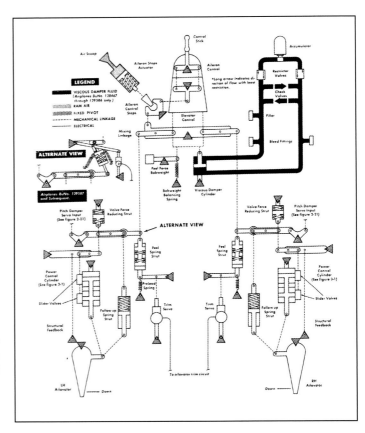

Ailevator control, feel, and trim system is necessary to cue artificial feel into the flight control system in order for the pilot not to overfly, thus overstressing the aircraft airframe. *Courtesy Author*

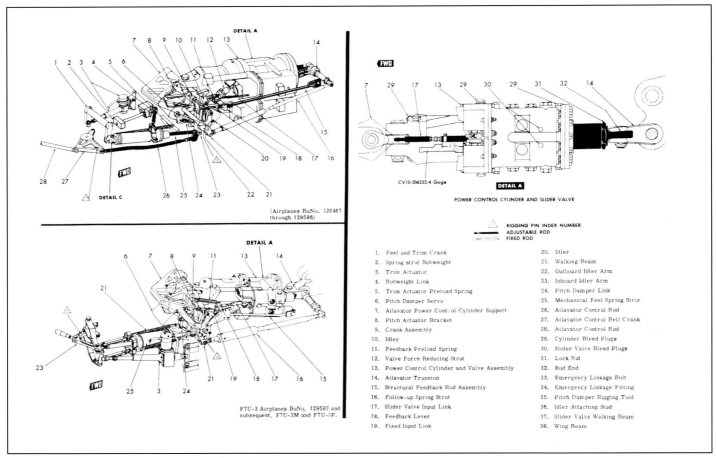

Rigging for all ailevator controls and subsequent power control compartment were responsible for ailevator activation. This artificial feel—cutting edge technology circa 1953—was very advanced and pragmatic from an endeavoring point of view. *Courtesy Author*

The aileron motion and functionality of the ailevators is predicated on restrictions placed upon it by an actual valve attached to a ram air scoop located on the underside of the fuselage. Ever increasing air pressure, due in part to the changing flight speed and through the changing position of the actual piston, and thus influenced by these events, restricts the movement of the entire assembly about its pivot point.

Ailevator motion is further controlled by a pitch servo which in turn is activated by the flight stabilization system. Also attached to the walking beam is the arm of the pitch servo via an idler assembly. The assembly remains at rest until it is momentarily actuated by the pitch servo. During the wing fold process the wing hinge pin assembly initiates the motion of a lever which places the idler into an obscurely shaped plate. This plate then locks a bell crank into the neutral position.

Ailevator Artificial Feel

With a mechanical simulated feel system, pilots would be enabled to proficiently fly their aircraft without the event of overstressing their vehicles due to inordinate ailevator deflection. Remember that, since the irreversible hydraulic control system fails to introduce a force reference at the control yoke a simulated feel is necessary for the pilots.

The actual feel is mechanically achieved though the combined efforts of the bob-weight, a bob-weight balancing spring, two mechanical spring struts, and a viscous damper. Viscous dampers oppose the direction of the motion with a force proportional to the rate of that motion. Bob-weights are connected to the control yoke through linkage, and functions only for that in longitudinal motions of the control stick, in relation to the vertical "G" loading. The bob-weight balancing spring neutralizes its own action for 1 "G" conditions. A viscous damper is connected directly to the control yoke and provides functionality for longitudinal motions of the control yoke. Spring struts positioned on each ailevator actuating cylinder provide feel in proportion to the movement of the ailevator. Proficient in both lateral and longitudinal motion, and in conjunction with the input linkage attachment to the actuating cylinder slider valves, they outline the critical design elements required to attain such a condition, that of artificial "feel."

Further enhancers to this system include a viscous damper circuit consisting of a damper cylinder, an accumulator, two one-way restrictors, two check relief valves, two bleed fittings, and finally, a check filler valve. The ensuing motion brought about by these enhancers is initiated from a cylinder piston and is dampened by the hydraulic fluid contained in the closed circuit.

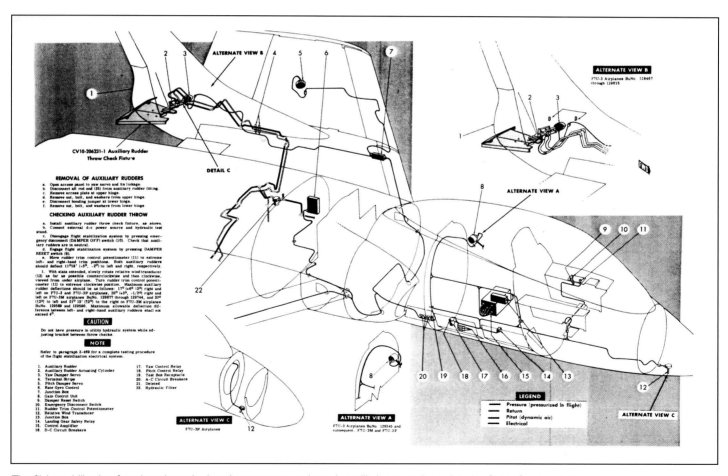

The flight stabilization found credence in damping out any aerodynamic oscillation experienced during flight. *Courtesy Author*

Flight Stabilization System

The flight stabilization system is designed to improve the stability of the aircraft as a gun platform and aids the pilot in the safe operation of the aircraft. Rudimentary flight stabilization systems were available for both the XF7U-1 and F7U-1, respectively. This improved system senses oscillations in pitch and in yaw through the pitch rate and yaw rate gyros located in the rate gyro control, and responds to these oscillations by sending the appropriate signals out. Adjusted through gain control and then amplified, these signals are routed to the proper servo such that the use of the auxiliary rudder and ailevators dampen the aircraft's oscillations. The yaw servos in turn control the slider valve or the rate thereof on the yaw cylinder. Through such control, the auxiliary rudders are activated for further dampening to occur. Likewise, the pitch servos activate the ailevator control linkage tied in tandem to the slider valves located on the ailevator actuating cylinders, further achieving dampening.

When slats are extended, a device known as a relative wind transducer senses the actual slip or skidding action of the aircraft and relays the proper electrical signals to the control amplifier. Here it is mixed and combined with the normal yaw damper signal, providing for increased directional stability. During slat extension, the pitch damper's functional system is interrupted and the pitch servos lock in neutral.

A rudder trim potentiometer is connected to the flight stabilization system to give the pilot direct control in trimming the auxiliary rudders around the aircraft's vertical axis. A rudder trim control resistor further aids in the control of the rudder trim potentiometer, thus ensuring good pilot control.

The Westinghouse J46-WE-8

The Westinghouse J46-WE-8, an outgrowth from the J34, has a marginal improvement from its predecessor. The J46, with its Westinghouse manufactured afterburner, provides roughly 5,800 lbs. of thrust in full afterburning, to which its J34 cousin supplied only 4,900 lbs. in the same mode. A margin of approximately 15.5% exists between contrasting designs.

The J46 essentially is an enlarged J34. The J34 sported a trim, 24 inch diameter, while the J46 entertains a marginal 5 inch increase in diameter, resulting in an overall diameter of 29 inches.

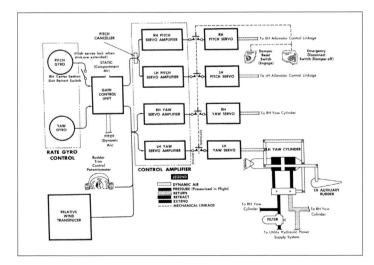

This flight stabilization electric schematic reveals the necessary components responsible for system functionality. *Courtesy Author*

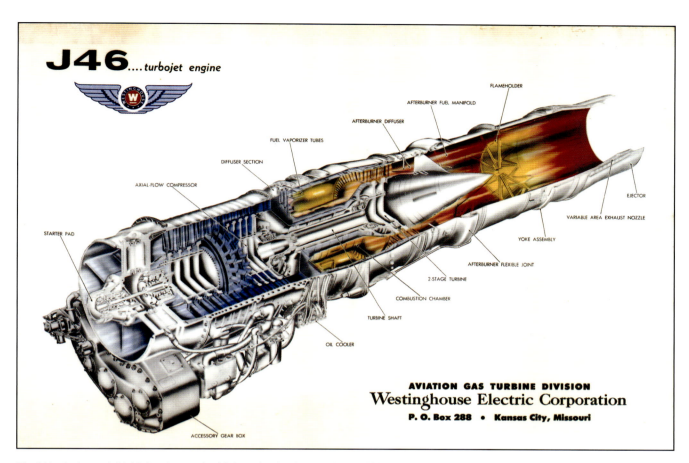

The Westinghouse J-46, big brother to the J 34, retained only a modest 15.5% overall increase in power to that of the J 34. This serious lack of thrust was never fully addressed, leaving an outstanding aircraft design to suffer unjustly. *Courtesy Author*

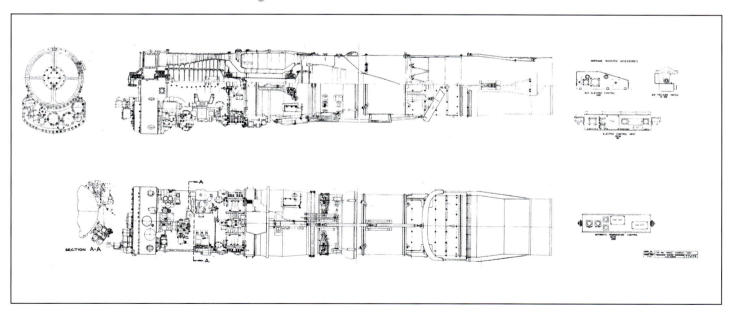

Every detail of the J 46, including afterburners, is outlined in this photo. Great care and preparation were invested in this turbojet design. *Courtesy Author*

The first F7U-3s were eventually powered by two Westinghouse J46-WE-8A turbojets, which quickly superseded the J46-WE-2 units originally slated for operation. After the 16th airframe manufactured the J46-WE-8A were quickly reverted to the 17th example onwards and would be the principal power plant for the Cutlass, and were the object of continuous upgrades.

The basic engine configuration consists of the same operational elements featured in the J34. The engine supports a single entry twelve stage axial flow compressor, a singular annular flow through combustion chamber, and a two stage turbine. The afterburner, with its accompanying controls, is manufactured by Westinghouse and is delivered as an integral unit with the turbojet.

This J 46-WE-8A, removed from Tom Cathcart's F7U-3 Cutlass, later fired up quite nicely through oiling and air cleaning of all exposed operating components. *Courtesy Tom Cathcart*

This photo illustrates both the engine and afterburners used in the F7U-3, F7U-3M, and 3P. Both J46 turbojets were installed first through use of quick change hardware built into the basic fuselage structure and then accommodated by the afterburners. *Courtesy Vought Hertiage Foundation*

Two J46 engines with afterburners are required to power the Cutlass, and are installed in the mid and aft fuselage sections of this vehicle. The engines are housed in adjoining compartments, one left and one right hand, and are supported by a centerline firewall. Both engines, unlike their XF7U-1 and F7U-1 predecessors, utilize a quick engine removal and installation; no longer is engine removal accessed from the aircraft's underside.

The engines are supported by engine mounts located on the inboard and outboard sides of each engine compartment at station 395. These mounts are of clamp design and are fabricated in two interlocking parts. Locking and unlocking are achieved by a spring loaded latch.

Two engine tracks are installed at the top of each engine compartment. Both tracks are comprised of a forward track and rearward track. The forward tract is secured to the upper fuselage bulkheads residing between stations 341 and 411. The rearward tracts are located between stations 456 and 468 and provide support for the afterburner. Both of these tracts, when conjoined with ground handling tracts, form a continuous support point, facilitating ease of removal. Only the rearward engine/afterburner support tract is not removable and retains a permanent fixture to that of the fuselage.

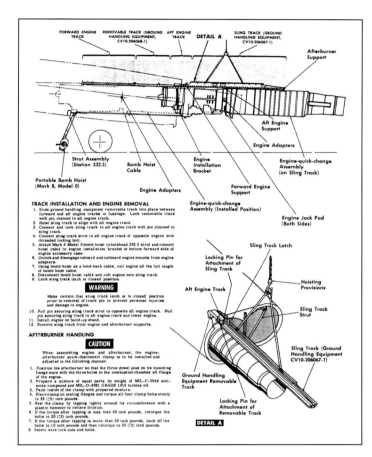

Unlike its F7U-1 predecessor, the F7U-3 incorporated the use of quick change engine assemblies that were reverted into its initial design phase. *Courtesy Author*

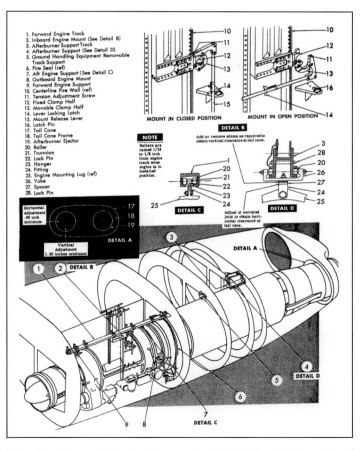

Internal hardware, rails, locks, etc. were strategically placed in the engine of the Cutlass. This helped necessitate often and infrequent engine changes experienced by the Cutlass during its operational life. *Courtesy Author*

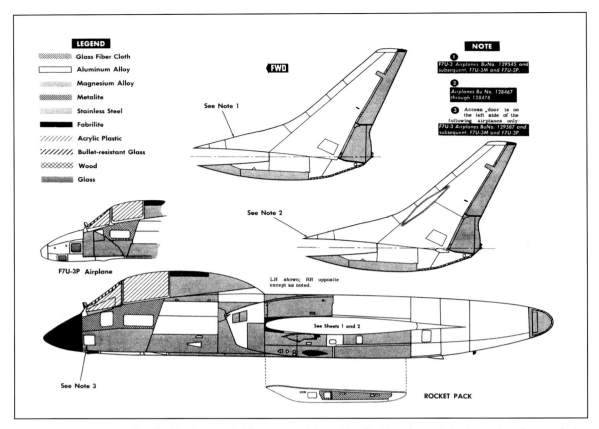

Fuselage skin plating is outlined in this photo, and different materials are identified by color and visual texturing. *Courtesy Author*

Afterburner and Other Supports

Engine supports are located on the top of the compressor inlet housing. Aft engine support is located on top of the engine diffuser section. The afterburner support projects through an opening approximately at the midpoint of this section and is secured into position, providing the necessary engine vertical support upon mounting.

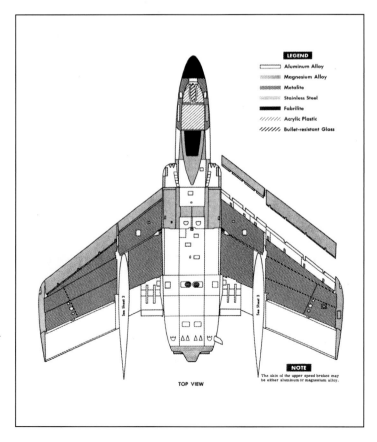

Top view of surface plating for the F7U-3. *Courtesy Author*

As the F7U-3 design matured into the F7U-3M (missile) and -3P (photographic) aircrafts, so did its weight. This would not be such a pressing issue or stumbling point for Vought engineers if it were not for the notoriously underpowered Westinghouse J34 and its newest J46 engines. Only when flying the Cutlass in full afterburner did its pilots gain appreciable insights into the aircraft's truest flight character. In spite of its jaded power plants, the Cutlass did outperform most of its contemporaries and will be discussed in length in the next chapter.

This F7U-3, relegated to a gate guardian, sports its external fuel tanks and is in relatively good condition. *Courtesy Author*

F7U-3 Buno No. 129596 shown with its hunched canopy in the open position and leading edge slats partially extended. *Courtesy William J Balogh*

Same F7U-3 from another viewing point; notice the dials barrier latch in front of the windscreen. *Courtesy William J Balogh*

This Cutlass did her deployment aboard the USS *Oriskany* (CVA-34) circa 1955 with VA 38, and can be seen here on display at an air show. *Courtesy National Naval Aviation Museum*

This unidentified gate guardian quietly poses, accentuating her fine aerodynamic lines to any curious observer. *Courtesy Author*

Chapter 7

F7U-3 Carrier Suitability Tests

The F7U-3 BU No. 128454, chosen as the first example for carrier suitability test, came from the first 16 original production block of 28 aircraft. The fourth airframe in the original series found its usefulness in shore based carrier tests in the clean configuration vigorously pursued by Chance Vought Aircraft and the Naval Air Test Center. Further tests were performed aboard the USS *Midway*, only to conclude off shore in varied states of configuration. Tests in the clean and stored configuration later culminated aboard the USS *Coral Sea*.

F7U-3 Buno 128454, number 4 of the first 16 produced in an initial production batch of 28 aircraft. Note dash one style of canopy while sporting newly designed radome. *Courtesy National Naval Aviation Museum*

Same aircraft without the apparent use of the left main wheel. The nose gear and oleo is completely turned 90° to the horizontal, displaying its use. *Courtesy National Naval Aviation Museum*

F7U-3 No. 128454 shown spotted on a catapult stationed on CVB-43, USS *Coral Sea*, for first set of carrier trails. *Courtesy Author*

First carrier trials: the same Cutlass being toweled to its catapult position by a mule. *Courtesy Author*

This test example was initially powered by Allison J35-A-29 non-afterburning turbojets, which were substituted in lieu of the unavailability of the Westinghouse J46-WE-2 engines with afterburners. This aircraft retained the catapulting and arresting geometry, power plant installation, and overall airframe design predominate in the first sixteen production examples while utilizing the radome and cockpit profiles evident on aircraft No. 17 onwards.

Subsequent testing on F7U-3 BU No. 128454 found relevance in two distinct configurations, Type A and Type B. The former, representative of the thrust line and center of gravity unique to that of the first sixteen production examples, would provide useful and coveted test data.

F7U-3 No. 128454 on the USS Coral Sea and shown in flight high above the Texas landscape and sporting the latest employed bulged canopy. Courtesy Jay Miller Collection

Further modifications to the airframe would yield the required thrust line and center of gravity renascent to that of the Type B configuration. The direct result of this act enabled the Cutlass to carry a 32-2.75" diameter rocket pack located on the fuselage centerline and up to two 2,000 lb. bombs, one positioned on each wing pylon.

The YF7U-3 BU No. 128471 (production example number 21 of 28 in the initial production batch) would be tested as well, revealing to Vought and BuAer some sobering and disconcerting results. Excerpts from the following test report reveal some distinct and prevalent shortcomings as regarding the No. 128471 article:

From: Commander, Naval Air Test Center
To: President, Board of Inspection and Survey
Subj: Project Ted No. BIS 21156, service acceptance trials of the model F7U-3 airplane, aircraft and engine performance tests; Letter report No. 2 Final report
References- Deleted
Introduction and Purpose
1. Service acceptance trials of the model F7U-3 airplane were established by "BuAer CONF LTR AER-AC-24 SER 05469 15 March 1952" with Project Ted No. BIS 21156, and a "B" priority assigned. Reference "BIS DISP 0313352 of February 1953" assigned model YF7U-3 airplane BU No. 128471 for the trials. This is the final letter report of the model F7U-3 airplane aircraft and engine performance tests which have been conducted by the flight test division of the Naval Air Test Center to determine performance for comparison with contract guarantees.

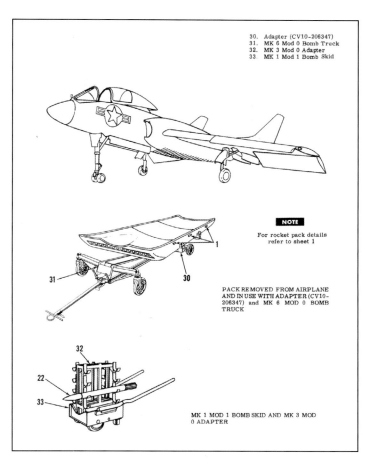

Diagram discussed how the rocket pack of 32 rockets is installed to the bottom side mid-fuselage. *Courtesy Author*

Cutlass BuNo. 128472, example 22 in the initial production batch of 28 aircraft, is almost identical to that of Cutlass no. 128471 cited in the book. *Courtesy Vought Heritage Foundation*

Starboard view of 128472 reveals the clean lines possessed by this aircraft. The length of the nose gear is evident and pronounced, further accentuating its distinct and unique appearance. *Courtesy Vought Heritage Foundation*

2. Because of maintenance difficulties encountered with model YF7U-3 BU No. 128471, additional data was obtained using model F7U-3 BU No. 129569 currently assigned to Project Ted No. PTR PP-6014.

Abbreviated Description of Test Aircraft

3. The model F7U-3 airplane is a single seat, swept-wing, tailless airplane equipped for land or carrier based operations and powered by two J46-WE-8B Westinghouse turbojet engines.

4. The test airplane was flown without external stores or pylons. Takeoff gross weight for YF7U-3 BU No. 128471 with full fuel was 27,360 lbs. at a CG position of 12.4% MAC (gear down) and 13.9% MAC (gear up).

Scope of Tests

5. Tests were conducted to obtain quantitative data for comparison with the following contract guarantees.

6. Stalling speed at sea level in full flight configuration at takeoff gross weight (1320 gallons of fuel) 108 KTS.

7. Rate of Climb at Takeoff Gross Weight (1320 gallons of fuel) with maximum thrust on a 95°F day at 115 KT with landing gear and slats extended guaranteed at 1650 FPM.

8. Service ceiling with normal thrust combat gross weight (792 gallons of fuel) guaranteed at 39,700 feet,

9. Maximum speed in level flight using military thrust with combat gross weight (792 gallons of fuel) guaranteed at 554 KT.

10. Weight empty guaranteed at 16,497 +100/-0.

11. In addition to the tests performed to determine compliance with contract guarantees, the following tests were conducted:

12. Minimum distance and obstacle type takeoffs

13. MRT climbs to service ceiling

14. Maximum airspeed in level flight at altitude using MRT

15. Weight empty, limited single engine performance evaluation, production system airspeed, and altimeter position errors, fuel quantity measuring system errors, and static thrust calibration of the engines installed in the airplane were determined during the preliminary evaluation phase of the tests.

16. All tests were conducted using gas turbine fuel MIL-F-5624A (JP-4).

Contract Guaranteed Items

17. The model F7U-3 airplane does not meet any of the contract guarantees. Table 7-1 sets forth the actual test results in relation to stipulated guarantees.

Stall Speeds

Port side quarter view highlights it' air intake, garnering further attention to its gun emplacements. No gun gas vents were as of yet introduced and subject to retrofitting. *Courtesy Vought Heritage Foundation*

18. The variation of stall speeds with gross weight for the model F7U-3 airplane in full flight configuration is given in Table 7-1. The stall speed in this configuration is at a CG of 13.0% MAC, and was determined to be 116 KT at sea level for the guaranteed weight of 28,090 lbs. as compared with the guaranteed value of 108 KT. With the landing gear and slats extended, a complete stall cannot be attained even with full aft stick.

Takeoff Rate of Climb

19. Actual data revealed a takeoff rate of climb to be 1,110 ft/min at 115 KT for an ambient temperature of 95°F and a gross weight of 28,090 lbs. as compared with the guaranteed value of 1,650 ft/min.

Climb Performance

20. Service ceiling with normal rated thrust was determined to be 34,450 ft at a guaranteed weight of 24,660 lbs. and standard atmospheric conditions as compared with the guaranteed value of 39,700 ft.

Level Flight Performance

21. Data indicated a maximum level flight speed of 505 KT at MRT was attained as compared with the guaranteed value of 554 KT.

Weight Empty

22. The actual weight empty of the model F7U-3 airplane was determined during the preliminary evaluation and was reported to be at 18,150 lbs. as compared with the guaranteed weight empty of 16,597 lbs.

Takeoff Performance

23. The minimum distance takeoffs were made with a technique not recommended for normal field takeoffs, thus the results should not be used for operational data. The recommended procedure for minimum field takeoff distance for the F7U-3 airplane is to pull the stick full aft smartly but smoothly, at 90-95 KTS IAS, and hold the stick aft until the airplane is airborne. Because of the satisfactory low speed handling characteristics of the model F7U-3 airplane, over rotation in pitch at takeoff is not critical. The average of the minimum distance type takeoffs performed was about 1,570 ft when corrected to standard sea level, no wind conditions at a gross weight of 28,090 lbs. Afterburners were used for all takeoff tests.

24. The technique used for the soft obstacle type takeoffs was similar to that for the minimum distance takeoffs. The application of aft stick was delayed until an airspeed of 100 to 105 KT IAS was attained, and the

Rear quarter starboard view denotes its twin vertical stabilizers, along with its subsequent ailevators and exhaust cone. *Courtesy Vought Heritage Foundation*

climb out was made at 115-120 KTS IAS. The average distance to clear a soft obstacle was 2,780 ft when corrected to standard sea level, no wind conditions at a gross weight of 28,090 lbs.

Airspeed and Altimeter Position Error

25. Airspeed and altimeter position error calibrations for the model F7U-3 airplane were duly noted and adjusted accordingly.

Conclusions

26. As a result of the aircraft and engine performance tests of the model F7U-3 airplane conducted under Project Ted No. BIS 21156, it is concluded:

A. The airplane fell short of meeting and of the revised contract guarantees.

B. The military rated thrust performance is unacceptably low.

C. Single engine performance is suitable only as an emergency measure.

D. The various discrepancies noted in the power plant and allied systems of the test airplane during the period of the trails represented a man-hour outlay considered excessive for an airplane of this type.

27. Based on the results of the preliminary evaluation of the model F7U-3, it is further concluded that:

A. The errors in the fuel quantity measuring system are unacceptably high.

B. The position errors of the production airspeed and altimeter system are unsatisfactory.

C. The cockpit instruments in the test airplane are inadequate for cruise control and a requirement exists for incorporation of a gross thrust meter and fuel flow indicator. Present plans call for correction of this discrepancy in all F7U-3 airplanes scheduled for delivery.

D. Aft and quartering visibility from the cockpit is unsatisfactory.

Recommendations

28. It is recommended that:

A. The model F7U-3 airplane not be accepted for service use

B. In future designs, consideration be given to avoid the deficiencies of the F7U-3 airplane reported here in.

Table 7-1
Model YF7U-3 Airplane BU No. 128471
Comparison of Performance Guarantees with
Actual Test Results

Guarantee Item	Guarantee Value	Test Result
Actual Weight Empty	16,497 +100/-0 lbs.	18,150 lbs.
Maximum Speed	554 KT	505 KT
Stalling Speed	108 KT	116 KT
Rate of Climb	1,650 FPM	1,110 FPM
Service Ceiling	39,700 ft	34,450 ft

Table 7-2

Model YF7U-3 Airplane BU No. 128471
Chronology of Tests and Major Maintenance Difficulties

Date of Original Test Directive
15 march 1952
Airplane BU No. 128471, received at N.A.T.C
1 Feb 1954
Broken nose wheel scissors and bent pre-rotation tube during towing at lightweight
2 March 1954
Test flying commenced, first flight aborted because of malfunctioning G-4 flight stabilization system
9 March 1954
Second flight aborted when radome nose section was lost on takeoff. Changed starboard engine as a result of internal damage
10 March 1954
All model F7U-3 airplanes grounded pending further investigation of spin recovery techniques
19 March 1954
Airplane in flying condition after repairing fuel and oil leaks, changing fuel control on new engine, resetting engine RPM and tailpipe temperatures and changing afterburner fuel control on port engine.
12 April 1954
All model F7U-3 airplanes at N.A.T.C grounded
16 April 1954
Test Flying Resumed
19 April 1954
Aircraft grounded for afterburner surging. Changed port afterburner because of cracked fuel manifold
20 April 1954
Flew engineering check flight. Afterburner surge still present. Auxiliary electric controls changed in both engines
3 May 1954
Test Flying Resumed
7 May 1954
All J46-WE-8B engines grounded for safety of operation inspection of oil pump
7 May 1954
Completed inspection, Airplane down for malfunctioning exhaust nozzle eyelids
21 May 1954
Test Flying Resumed
26 May 1954
Airplane down for low turbine out temperatures as gas leak
26 May 1954
Test Flying Resumed
28 May 1954
Completed preliminary evaluation flying
1 June 1954
Calibrated turbine out temperature
8 June 1954
Burnt wiring in nose wheel well circuit breaker panel
21 June 1954
Test Flying Resumed
24 June 1954

Afterburner nozzle bent on port engine
1 July 1954
Flying Resumed
9 July 1954
Strengthened tail cone and fuel access doors
12 July 1954
Hydraulic leak in starboard wing ailavator power cylinder
13 July 1954
Flying Resumed
16 July 1954
Down for calendar check and instruments for measured takeoffs
21 July 1954
Airplane AOG for fuel pump parts
27 July – 9 Aug 1954
Airplane AOG for hydraulic lien
9 Aug – 25 Aug 1954
Unable to obtain engine start
7 Sept `954
Replaced burned out starter on starboard engine
8 Sept 1954
Down for fuel leak
10 Sept 1954
Flying Resumed
17 Sept 1954
Down for fuel leak
24 Sept 1954
Flying Resumed
25 Sept 1954
Down for fuel leak in underside fueling manifold
28 Sept 1954
Down to replace aluminum wiring with copper wire. Safety of flight
28 Sept 1954
AOG for fuel boost pump
8 Oct – 14 Oct 1954
Main inverter replaced
18 Oct – 26 Oct 1954
Flying Resumed
27 Oct 1954
Project Flying Completed
12 Nov 1954

Second Carrier Suitability Trials

The second set of carrier suitability trials highlights were the use of significantly modified YF7U-3 BU No. 128475 to the extent and proficient testing of this example aboard the USS *Coral Sea* (CUA-43), USS *Lake Champlain* (CUA-39), and the USS *Hancock* (CUA-19). Tests were also levied at the Naval Air Test Center and the Naval Air Material Center. Accompanying the Cutlass No. 128475 aboard the USS *Hancock* were the YF7U-3 Cutlass BU Nos. 129552 and 129638 to explore and evaluate the effectiveness of the C-11 steam catapult and the MK7 modi-arresting gear. The Cutlass No. 129567 was assigned in turn and specifically used for barrier testing.

The YF7U-3 BU No. 128475, maintaining its place of being the 25th production example in the initial production batch, possessed the distinction of employing lessons learned from the first series of carrier tests in its overall design architecture and would embrace the following upgrades. Power plant changes would include the incorporation of the Westinghouse J46-WE-8A engines from its former J35-A-29 turbojet. A pilot steerable dual nose wheel would aid aircraft on deck handling characteristics. Airframe weight was reduced, and the arresting hook design changed as well. The fuel tank was modified to reduce the amount of trapped fuel in the fuel transfer process during flight. The wing pylon was significantly strengthened in order to carry heavier ordinance. Power control changes were initiated to reduce pilot error. The arresting gear strength would reduce from 4.55 G at 22,765 lbs. to that of 4.2 G at 21,065 lbs. Maximum arresting weight would be reduced from 26,180 lbs to 24,200 lbs. Barrier ultimate strength would be reduced from 5.8G at 22,765 lbs to that of 5.45 G at 21,065 lbs.

In accordance with and alluded to, a chronological progression of tests would provide the following:

Record of Tests
Date
Test Initialization Date
15 March 1952
Aircraft Arrival
28 September 1953
Tests Begin
1 October 1953
Tests Aboard the USS Coral Sea
26 – 30 October 1953
Airframe and Power Plant Maintenance
18 November 1953
Testing Re-Initiated
15 January 1954
Testing Progressed Aboard the USS Lake Champlain
8 – 13 February 1954
Aircraft Hydraulic Maintenance
24 February 1954
Tests Re-Initiated
14 March 1954
Airplane Grounded Again
19 March 1954
Tests Resume
18 April 1954
Tests Placed at the Naval Air Material Center
5 May 1954
Tests Aboard the USS Hancock
14 June – 30 July 1954
Barrier Tests Begin
24 – 30 August 1954
Tests Are Concluded
12 October 1954

F7U-3 BuNo 129662 from project Cutlass demonstrates how the Cutlass achieved flight at the end of the carrier deck involving a steam catapult. *Courtesy Vought Heritage Foundation*

F7U-3 NATC USS *Coral Sea* (CV-93) wears its subsequent catapulting cable with pride. *Courtesy National Naval Aviation*

F7U-3 Buno 13 9897 is being spotted on a steam catapult on CVA 55's angled carrier deck circa June 1957. *Courtesy Vought Hertiage Foundation*

The entire catapulting system, as well as the arrestor system were evaluated, along with the entire Cutlass program, producing the following results:

Catapulting

Type	No. of Catapults	Location
H4B	61	N.A.T.C
H8	26	N.A.T.C
H4-1	14	USS *Coral Sea*
H8	21	USS *Lake Champlain*
XC-11	7	N.A.M.C
C-11	35	USS *Hancock*

Arrested Landings Results Thereof:

Engine and Reeving	Wire Size	No. of Landings	Location
MK5, 20:1 (2 engine)	1 inch	55	N.A.T.C
MK5, 24:1 (2 engine)	1.125 inch	5	N.A.T.C
MK.5, 24:1 (2 engine)	1.375 inch	8	N.A.T.C
MK7, 28:1 (2 engine)	1.125 inch	12	N.A.T.C
MK7, 28:1 (2 engine)	1.375 inch	14	N.A.T.C
MK5, 12:1	1 inch	13	USS Coral Sea
MK5, 12:1	1 inch	20	USS Lake Champlain
MK7, 18:1	1.375 inch	33	USS Hancock

Unidentified F7U-3 with tail hook fully extended. Note in-flight refueling boom portraying from the radome. *Courtesy Vought Hertiage Foundation*

Summary of Tests With Conclusions

It was determined that the following characteristics were found most prevalent in the F7U-3 Cutlass BU No. 128475. Cockpit access was particularly hazardous, especially during high wind conditions when the access ladder wasn't employed. Problems with head rest positioning were encountered, along with lower seat positioning than actually desired. The maximum power lever was mostly out of reach from the typical pilot, further obscuring the landing gear and slats position indicator from apparent view. Adding insult to injury, the wing fold lock could not be located by touch. The cockpit lighting, along with its range intensity, was deemed adequate.

The catapult accessories specified in paragraph 21 were found to be acceptable for use of the catapults so indicated. Another catapult related item, the holdback socket installation CV10-654051-1, was unsatisfactory but acceptable. The airplane must be positioned on the H-8 or C-11 type catapult within three inches of center when launching with asymmetrical load. The catapulting launch characteristics in regards to the H4B, H4-1, H-8, and C-11 when in use were found to be satisfactory. The nose wheel steering mechanism, deemed an asset when taxiing the vehicle to launch position, should be disengaged when towed by a mule tractor support vehicle.

F7U-3 on final approach with arrestor hook fully extended aboard CVA-19, USS *Hancock*. *Courtesy Vought Hertiage Foundation*

Same Cutlass making contact with the arrestor cable, providing a safe and successful landing. *Courtesy Vought Hertiage Foundation*

F7U-3 Cutlass from VF-124 displays 409/D with wings folded and undergoing a preflight inspection by the pilot. *Courtesy Vought Hertiage Foundation*

The production arresting hook actuating cylinder assembly, CV10-601023-1 and -2, were found unacceptable. Likewise, the abovementioned actuating cylinder assembly was modified to accept a relief valve to operate an 800 psi air pressure assembly and found to be satisfactory. In a structural sense the loads imposed, especially at fuselage station 437 from the arresting hook, were determined unacceptable. With the incorporation of EP303 in reinforcing from 437 it was still found unacceptable. Through modification of the CV10-601045 to the entire actuating cylinder and circuit and the proper bulkhead reinforcement to frame 437 they eventually found complete acceptance in this regard. Later on, hook bounce experienced with the arresting hook actuating cylinder equipped with a .102 inch diameter orifice was found unacceptable.

The main landing gear wheel, GY9560201, was found satisfactory when utilizing a tire pressure of 280 psi. The main gear tire pressures, ascertained to be 240 psi for main wheels and 280 psi for nose wheels, were found adequate both on a fixed runway and aboard a carrier deck sporting 1 inch diameter pendants, but not so on carrier decks affixed to 1.375 inch diameter deck pendants. This was in alliance with the MK5 arresting gear.

Single engine carrier approaches on landing were dicey at best and deemed unacceptable. The lag in the longitudinal trim system wasn't acceptable due to flaws in the leveling procedures for weight and balance. Errors found in fuel gauge accuracy were uncovered, along with the aft towing bar being considered virtually useless.

Cutlass 409/D with wings extended awaits its turn on the catapult aboard CVA-19, USS *Hancock*. *Courtesy The National Naval Aviation Museum*

Miscellaneous Items

The fuel vent system allows the transfer of fuel, eventually overfilling the aft fuselage tank. On the same note, the air intake nose duct wall strength, or lack thereof, was found inadequate. The strength of the tail cone has become an issue. The fuel booster pump West 22E694-10 is unfit for use. The barrier detent CV10-444067-1 improperly deployed consistently for proper barrier cable activation to take place and is therefore deemed useless.

Recommendations

In spite of all short comings found, it was recommended that the F7U-3 airplane be accepted for service with the immediate exception of limiting the Cutlass to land bases, in lieu of the apparent structural workings found at fuselage station 437. Full service activation would be achieved upon the incorporation of the new arresting hook actuating cylinders and the proper structural modifications to the bulkhead at fuselage station 437. Other elements provided in the recommendations would include the improved use of a fuel quantity measuring system and a hold back socket installation for one hand operation. It was also recommended that the landing gear and slats position indicator be relocated for better accessibility, while the seat headrest needed to be made more accessible, especially during catapulting. Also included was compliance to catapulting accessories outlined in paragraph 21 and readied and accepted for use. Cockpit lighting was a pressing issue only to be addressed by the improvement of certain instrumentation and assorted lighting installations.

It was strongly recommended that an auxiliary light be installed on the right wing tip in assistance to the LSO officer during night carrier landings. Other, more salient improvements would include improving the vertical fin stub skid service life, improving upon the barrier detent strength, and providing a fuel vent system that prevented the overfilling of the aft fuselage tank. Finally, provisions would be made to remove the fuel booster pumps and make available a more visible trim position switch, especially during night operations.

Project Cutlass

The U.S. Navy initiated the fleet introduction program at NAS Patuxent River, Maryland. Soon after the F7U-3 completed its required tenure, Project Cutlass was established. This was set up to evaluate the Cutlass under operational conditions in order to form the contingent of the West Coast's first operational squadron. The first Cutlass, BU No. 128466, arrived at NAS Miramar, CA, on 2 February 1954 at the hands of LCDR R.G. Puckeit and was aptly turned over to LCDR J.S. Brown, the officer in charge of Project Cutlass. Eventually the program would amass a dozen aircraft, all of which qualified aboard the USS *Hancock*. After copious amounts of touch-and-goes the ranks of aircraft would soon thin. Six aircraft accompanied by LTs Schirra, Shelton, and Sheppard were transferred to Moffett Field to eventually form VC-3.

Flight Characteristics

General- The low aspect ratio swept-wing orientation provided excellent stability and control characteristics throughout its speed range. Wing slats provided good speed control during level flight and in dives.

Stalls, especially with gear down and slats extended, were preceded by mild rudder buffeting. If the aircraft's center of gravity was too far forward, the plane gently pitched down during this stall. There was the absence of any tendency of yawing or rolling with the ailevator action fully functional.

Spins. The tendency for the F7U-3 to spin will be discussed in greater length in Chapter 9 under the Cornell University study.

Angle of Bank Gross Weight	0°	15°	30°	45°
Takeoff Condition				
32,000 lbs	121	123	130	144
28,000 lbs	113	115	122	135
24,000 lbs	105	107	113	125
Cruise Condition				
30,000 lbs	133	135	142	158
26,000 lbs	123	126	133	147
22,000 lbs	113	116	122	135
Landing Condition				
28,000 lbs	113	115	122	135
24,000 lbs	105	107	113	125
20,000 lbs	96	98	103	114

Inverted Spins

Data on inverted spins is not available. It is anticipated that such a condition could transpire since available down elevator is insufficient to trim the airplane.

Spin Recovery

Should a pilot encounter a spin early on it was thought that the Cutlass couldn't be spun; it was recommended that relinquishing all control inputs during the spin would aid in the eventual recovery from such a condition. If the vehicle was fully laden with external ordinance and stores it was strongly recommended to jettison the entire load in the aid for full recovery.

Flight Controls

Ailavators were the primary control mechanism for lateral and longitudinal movement initiated by the proper control inputs from the pilot. Fore and aft stick motions produced vertical motions on the control surface initiating pitch. Lateral motions on the stick induce rolling motion, and very high at around 540° per second. The Cutlass had a tendency at around Mach .88 for the nose to tuck under, which was aptly corrected by the appropriate trimming. Higher speeds do produce higher stick forces, and were accurately portrayed by the artificial feel system.

Rudder control, trim control auxiliary rudder, and flight stabilization systems all functioned in concert to dampen directional or longitudinal oscillations produced and were exclusively inherent to that of the Cutlass design.

Level Flight Characteristics

Low speed handling included a stall that exhibited good handling qualities. The main difference between this design as compared to that of a more conventional design lies in its unusual higher angle of attack required for takeoff and landing.

High Speed Flight

This aircraft, because of its unique design, was capable of very high speeds and rates of climb, and demonstrated excellent overall control characteristics through the transonic region. Stability remained excellent up to and including Mach 0.88; above this number would require higher stick forces for the added control. Speed brakes were used in moderate dives up to speeds including 480 knots.

F7U-3M Buno 139894 from VA 86 basks in the sun at an unidentified Naval Air Station. *Courtesy National Naval Aviation Museum*

Cutlass 407/D, 410/D, 405/D, 401/D, and 409/D retain their respectful positions along the edge of the flight deck belonging to CVA-19 USS *Hancock*, September 1955. *Courtesy Vought Hertiage Foundation*

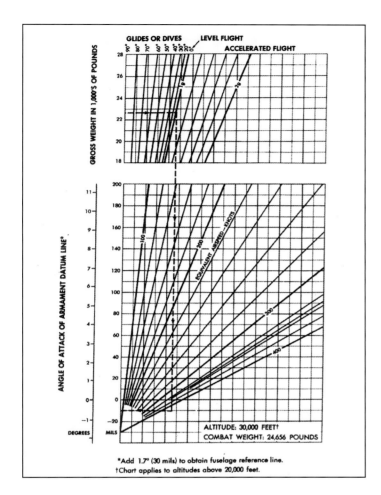

Flight charts to aid the pilot in weight and angle of attack issues before and during flight. *Courtesy Author*

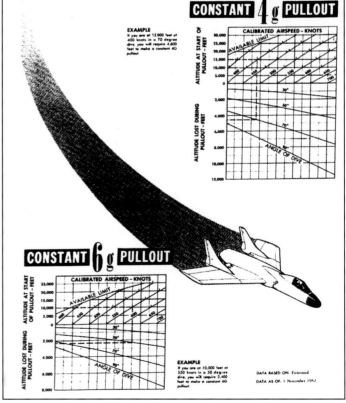

Flight charts for altitude airspeed relationships for 4g and 6g constant pull outs. *Courtesy Author*

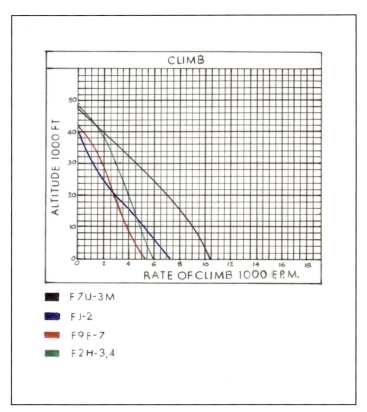

Rate of climb chart involving the North American FJ-2 Grumman F9F-7 and McDonnell F2H-3, with performance summaries in relation to that of the F7U-3M. All candidates fall within the rate of climb envelopes of that of the Cutlass. It is clear that the Cutlass was superior to its contemporaries in rate of climb and other flight characteristics as well. *Courtesy Author*

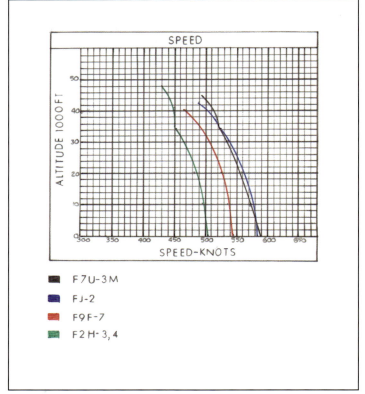

Speeds at altitude, here again involving the North American FJ-2, Grumman F9F-7, and McDonnell F2H-3 and -4 in comparison to that of the Cutlass. The Cutlass far outclassed the F9F-7 and F2H-3 and -4, but was marginalized somewhat by the FJ-2. Still, in all the Cutlass fared the better and could have pursued a much more robust flight envelope if not suffering from its under-powered turbojets. *Courtesy Author*

F2H-3 Banshee on final approach to (CVA -11) USS Intrepid circa 1952. *Courtesy Author*

Grumman F9F-7 and North American FJ 2 Fury parked along the edge of the aft flight deck aboard CVA-11 USS Intrepid circa 1952. *Courtesy Author*

Chapter 8

Cutlass Versatility

The Cutlass underwent a tactical metamorphosis, so to speak, and found relevance in significantly more proposals. The F7U-3 basic airframe found credence in the following roles:

Fighter airplane (F7U-3) – Gun or air-to-air rocker
Attack airplane (A2U-1)-7 Pylon Stations
Sparrow 1 Missile Carrier (F7U-3M)
Photo Graphic Airplane (F7U-3P)
Flight Refueling
Aero 14A Spray Tanks

The basic airframe design configuration lends itself quite readily to the abovementioned applications. Chance Vought engineers investigated, evaluated, and determined that the basic design of the F7U-3 possessed far more potential than once thought. This design provided the use of special hard points and allowed to facilitate the use of external stores like gravity bombs, more fuel tanks, a 2.75 FAR Rocket pack, and eventually the sparrow 1 guided air-to-air missile. Investigations of aircraft flight and handling characteristics involving up to and including 3,500 pounds of external ordnance proved to be satisfactory, and overall aircraft speed was unencumbered as well.

The F7U-3, as well as other variations of this basic design, employed the use of at least thirty-two "2.75" FAR rockets located in a dispersal pod on the underside of the fuselage.

This pack was easily secured or detached by the activation of six pins firmly routed in retractable female fittings in the fuselage. Re-acquisition or installation of the rockets in their respective pack were easily attainable, especially from the front and rear bank of the pod, without removal from the fuselage under structure. The rocket pod dispenser sequence was solely governed by the MK16 fire control system. Along with its four 20 mm cannon it provided the entire offensive power deployed in the F7U-3 design. The F7U-3 only possessed two inner wing pylons, used exclusively for external fuel tankage.

Port side view of this pristine F7U-3M illustrates and punctuates its stark beauty. Leading edge slats partially extended pronounce its full functionality. *National Naval Aviation Museum*

A2U-1

Vought, in 1951, proposed to the Navy its U-389, or A2U-1 (attack) version of the F7U-3 predicated upon its existing design. The A2U-1 would include seven pylon stations, and could carry up to 7,000 lbs of ordinance or seven 19 round rocket packs totaling 133 rounds of "2.75" FAR rockets. Other design highlights would include the J46-WE-18 engines yet to be developed, and two 20 mm cannon instead of four, augmented by a new electronics and gun control system. Provisions would be made to include more fuel cells, topping internal fuel capacity to 1,672 gallons or 10,868 lbs of JP-4. Total weight of this fully loaded aircraft would dwell around a robust 29,375 lbs. Any significant weight increase would be offset by the more powerful Westinghouse turbojets. The Navy would eventually lose interest and cancel the contract on 18 November 1954.

F7U-3M, "The Missile Carrier"

The F7U-3M "M," for missile, remained essentially the same as its cousin, the F7U-3, in overall dimensional stature. The prevailing and signature difference lay in its ability to operate the Sparrow 1 missile in air-to-air operations, and made available provisions for the for the additional inclusion of two 124 gallon wing tanks and four wing pylons. The Aero 10E Armament Control System, which is used for the guidance of the Sparrow 1 missiles, contains the following elements. This system consists of the AN/APQ-51 radar augmented by the MK 16 mod 4 fire control system.

F7U-3 fitted with a delta tip ailevator once slated for the still born A2U-1. Vought, through the eyes of its engineers, envisioned and negotiated with the U.S. Navy for an expanded role for the F7U-3 airframe. *Courtesy Jay Miller Collection*

F7U-3M BuNo 129655 resides at the National Naval Aviation Museum and is an excellent restoration of this aircraft. This is how a finished Cutlass in Naval colors appears. *Courtesy National Naval Aviation Museum*

The nose gear oleo strut garnered much negative attention due to the fact that it possessed a rather nasty habit of collapsing during a hard landing. Some struts would transit through their mounts and introduce themselves to their pilots via the ejection seat. *Courtesy National Naval Aviation Museum*

Forward nose gear oleo strut wheel well is vary spacious, and structurally sound, affording the need of the radial area for wheel pre-rotation. *Courtesy National Naval Aviation Museum*

Starboard side intake sports a boundary layer fence directing the ensuring air flow to its Westinghouse J46-WE-8A engine. Two were used in all. Above the intake resides two 20mm cannon accompanied by their respecting gun gas vents. *Courtesy National Naval Aviation Museum*

Starboard side inner wing panel leading edge slat partially extended sports generous amounts of red primer. Zinc chromate primer was initially used early on in the Cutlass program, eventually being superceded by the former. *Courtesy National Naval Aviation Museum*

Cross section view of in board leading edge slat denoted extension arms and attachment points to the wing. The air foil shape virtually details the directed air flow over the top of the wing, influencing lift at high angles of attack. *Courtesy National Naval Aviation Museum*

Outer wing panel leading edge slat fully exposed also accents the wing fold mechanism and locking apparatus. *Courtesy National Naval Aviation Museum*

F7U-3 Cutlass numbers 129589 and 129590 were converted into F7U-3M prototypes, to which 98 examples were eventually ordered, culminating in first flight of a production F7U-3M on 12 July 1954. Tests subsequently performed on this newest example of the Cutlass provided noteworthy results, indicating no adverse effects in regards to its handling qualities during flight with the missiles present. The missiles were installed on launchers sporting 3 foot long launch rails for the advent of normal operations. A cartridge release enabled the quick disconnect of all missiles in the event of an emergency. When carrying missiles the guns and ammunition may be removed, further initiating a reduction in weight without significantly altering the vehicles' balance.

The F7U-3M was also equipped with outer wing panel fuel cells and was quite capable of carrying any of the munitions and stores that the basic F7U-3 airframe carried.

The basic board or aim 9 sidewinder missile utilizing infra-red homing could also be reverted to the F7U-3 basic airframe. This proved the adaptability of the F7U-3 aircraft, and because this missile is infra-red and not radar homing complicated radar equipment could be excluded, further benefiting weight reduction.

Outer wing panel at 90° fold line next to starboard vertical stabilizer emphasizes this aircraft's overall compactness required for storage below deck on Essex and midway class aircraft carriers. *Courtesy National Naval Aviation Museum*

Fuel vent shown and is highlighted by the starboard engine exhaust cone. Early cones were mechanically actuated by the pilot, later to be controlled by the pilot and accessories section of the turbojet. *Courtesy National Naval Aviation Museum*

Port side main landing gear oleo strut and wheel are of Vought design and imply the shear strength and stoutness of its appearance. *Courtesy National Naval Aviation Museum*

Port side inner wing panel leading edge slat partially extended displays the red primer as well. *Courtesy National Naval Aviation Museum*

Calm shell speed brake slightly opened was an effective device for air speed management. *Courtesy Author*

Port side view exposing 90° wing fold and partially extended slat. *Courtesy National Naval Aviation Museum*

Cockpit tub of the F7U-3M highlights the control yoke and rudder pedals, accentuated by the control panel sporting a gyro compass and turn and bank indicator. *Courtesy National Naval Aviation Museum*

This is the gun sight used in conjunction with the MK16 mod 4 fire control system in the F7U-3M cockpit. *Courtesy National Naval Aviation Museum*

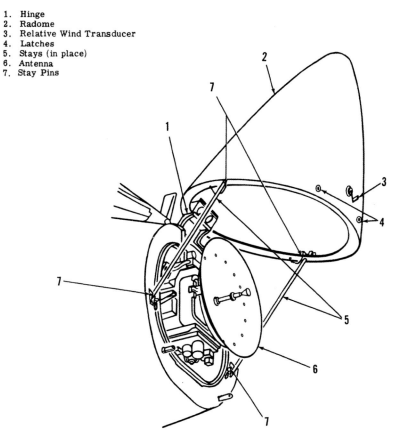

1. Hinge
2. Radome
3. Relative Wind Transducer
4. Latches
5. Stays (in place)
6. Antenna
7. Stay Pins

TO OPEN F7U-3M RADOME

a. Release latches (4).
b. Raise radome (2) to fully open position and support radome.
c. Remove radome support stays (5) from stowage areas.
d. Install stays and secure with stay pins (7).

TO REMOVE F7U-3M RADOME

a. Remove radome support stays from stowed position in RH main gear wheel well.
b. Release radome latches (4).
c. Raise radome, install stays (5) and secure with pins (7).
d. Disconnect electrical leads at terminal strip in top of radome (2).
e. Remove stays (5).
f. With radome properly supported, remove radome hinge pin.
g. Carefully guide radome forward over radar equipment.

CAUTION

When removing or installing radome make sure it clears the radar antenna (6). Do not scratch or mar the radome as the efficiency of the radar will be decreased.

The AN/APQ-51 radar and ranging system was quite sophisticated for its time and boasted a rather high degree of reliability and dependability and ushered in the all missile era Naval jet fighters. *Courtesy Author*

Front view of the photographic Cutlass shows its unusual nose, configured for cameras for reconnaissance purposes, which was eventually relegated to research purposes. *Courtesy Author*

The F7U-3P (Photographic)

Approximately the same time the F7U-3M was ordered the Navy also requested 12 examples of the F7U-3P Cutlass predicated on the existing F7U-3 airframe with the extension of the nose by 25 inches; photographic equipment could then be installed atop the fuselage behind the cockpit. First flight for the F7U-3P occurred 1 July 1954 without apparent incident.

Four major types of photographic missions were envisioned for this newest derivative of the Cutlass: general reconnaissance; reconnaissance mapping and charting; beach, amphibious, and offshore reconnaissance; and night reconnaissance.

They were all accommodated by the interchanging of various cameras and their respective mounts.

Port side view of the photographic Cutlass concentrates on the modified nose housing the cameras. *Courtesy Author*

Starboard side glance suggest its ugly ducking appearance. *Courtesy Author*

Port side view of an F7U-3P Cutlass sunning itself. *Courtesy Author*

Forward view of the cockpit tub reveals the intrinsic complexity involved in its overall design. The F7U-3P, devoid of any armament, was supplanted with supporting photographic equipment. *Courtesy Author*

This unidentified F7U-3P supports the use of Fletcher auxiliary fuel tanks. *Courtesy Jay Miller Collection*

Another view of an unidentified F7U-3P Cutlass. Notice its two oblique camera windows located in the lower nose section. *Courtesy Author*

Located aft of the cameras, just above the cockpit instrument panel, resided the photographic view finder. This device afforded the forward and vertical viewing to the pilot via a viewing lens. By virtue of this instrumentation it allowed the pilot to adjust and set the cameras through specific cockpit controls, adjust the interval controller, and film speed, especially of the beach reconnaissance cameras. Normal camera operation was routinely an automatic process devoid of any pilot participation. Azimuth control was facilitated to enable the pilot to orientate the camera with the aircraft's line of flight. Equipment would include:

Gerenal reconnaissance
FWD Bay….P-2 Strike Camera
Station # 1 ….K-17
Station # 2 ….K-17 ORK 38 Fixed Or Rot/Mount
Mapping or Charting
FWD Bay -----
Station # 1 …..K17 ORCA-8 ORT-11
Station # 2 …...K17 OR CA-8 ORT-11 TRI-MET
Beach and offshore reconnaissance
FWD Bay----
Station # 1---- Shutter Trip Control
Station # 2---- K—37
Azimuth Instillation
FWD Bay -------
Station # 1 …..K17-C Or Cas 2 Azimuth Rotation
Station #2 …..K17-C Or Cas 2 Azimuth Rotation
General Reconnaissance-Forward Firing
FWD Bay And---
Station # 1 ……K38-Forward Firing
Station # 2 ……K17

As time would allow all 12 examples of the F7U-3P were reverted for evaluation purposes only.

F7U-3P BuNo 129745 in flight. Nose appears to be red in actual color photo. *Courtesy Jay Miller Collection*

F7U-3P BuNo 129745 in a short left turn sports an instrumentation boom on the left side wing tip. *Courtesy Author*

Special Store Carrier

The F7U-3 design configuration allowed for the installation of a number of special stores located on the center section pylon. This store employed ample ground clearance during catapulting and landing. Great thought went into the aerodynamic, structural, and carrier suitability design constraints dictated by the F7U-3's existing operational environment, demonstrating four differentiating types of stores carried by Vought's design bomb ejector rack. All four stores were successfully carried and separated without any adverse effects.

Some separation of stores was achieved at supersonic speeds. This aircraft would further earn distinction by being the first in service aircraft to do so.

The 29th and subsequent F7U-3s, as well as the 1st and subsequent A2U-1s before cancellation, had provisions for the installation of the 18 A (LABS) low altitude bombing system. Conversion kits needed for this very purpose would include the FE-T-145 control box, ejector rack, wiring harness, and MC 215 actuator, located on the left hand center section pylon. The T 44 range selector and jumper harness were found in the right hand electronics compartment.

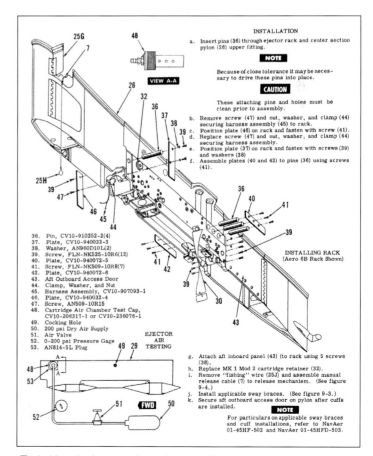

Typical bomb ejector rack used on special stores at hard points on the wing of the F7U-3. *Courtesy Author*

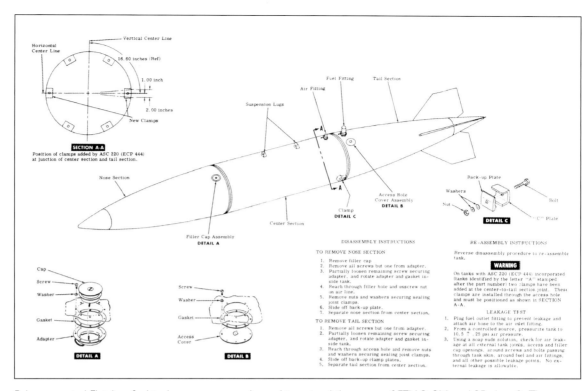

Pylon mounted Fletcher fuel tanks were commonly used to extend the range of F7U-3, 3M, and 3P aircraft. They were quite aerodynamic and easy to use. *Courtesy Author*

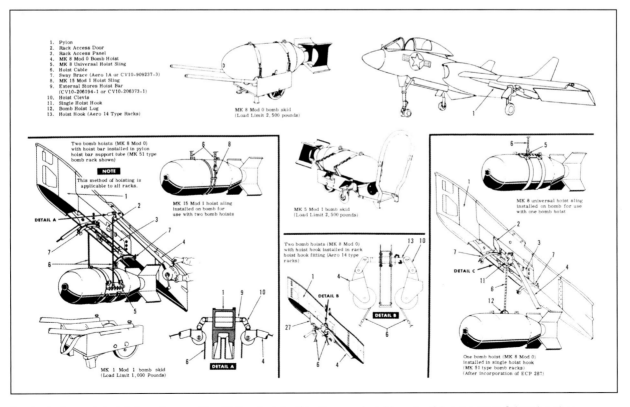

Bomb ejector rack installation diagram. The Cutlass lent itself to the an adaptable potential as a potent fighter-bomber. *Courtesy Author*

In-flight Refueling

Provisions were made to modify every fourth F7U-3 to accept in-flight refueling equipment. In-flight refueling tests were successfully performed between a F7U-3 and its A J tanker at altitudes between 5,000 and 25,000 feet. This in-flight system allowed the refueling of the F7U-3 while in flight. This was accomplished through the activation and engagement of the in-flight refueling probe and subsequent drogue. There were no provisions for refueling the F7U 3P aircraft in flight.

Vought endeavored to modify some current F7U-3 airframes by equipping them with an "A Buddy" refueling tank. The sheer nature of the act allowed the F7U-3 to be refueled by tanker versions of this same aircraft.

Reasons cited for this decision reside in the fact that the latter would posses the same speed and flight characteristics as the refueling aircraft, thus negating dangerously lower merging speeds with slower piston/propeller driven tankers employed at the time.

F7U-3M Cutlass Bu No. 129655 sported an in-flight refueling probe located at the tip of the radome.
Courtesy National Naval Aviation Museum

Same aircraft different view. Notice the off-set of the probe from deep center. *Courtesy National Naval Aviation Museum*

This port side view of the same aircraft delineates the actual length of the boom, supporting sufficient length to engage the refueling drogue and providing the necessary connectivity for fuel transfer to take place. *Courtesy National Naval Air Museum*

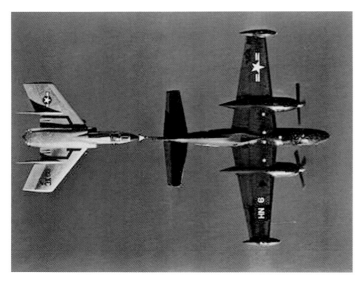

VX-3 F7U-3 129643 in the process of receiving fuel from an AJ-2 Savage Aerial Tanker. *Courtesy Author*

The buddy aerial refueling system, as it was eventually known, involved the addition to the existing airframe of a 150 gallon center line fuel tank located on the left pylon accompanied by a 220 gallon center line fuel pod accentuated by a 150 gallon "Buddy" refueling tank equipped with a boom supported drogue. This type of refueling increased the range of existing F7U-3s from 285 to 500 nautical miles with the special inclusion of the 150 gallon fuel tank, a fuel pod, and a special store. Previsions were made to accommodate the A2U-1 before its contract cancellation.

Aero 14 A Spray Tanks

Design modifications were made to the F7U-3 and A2U-1, allowing them to carry the aero 14A spray tank. A Chance Vought ejector rack designed to carry these tanks was tested at flight speeds up to and including 570 knots EAS without experiencing any aberrant effects. Prototype evaluations indicated satisfactory spray characteristics. The following summary of equipment that played significant roles in the various developmental phases of these aircraft is as follows:

Same aircraft involved viewed from the starboard side. *Courtesy Author*

F7U-3
F7U-3M
F7U-3P
  Power Plant Configuration
A2U-1

Engines	Installed in airplane	Max/Rated/Thrust	Crusing SFC
Allison J35-A-29	F7U-3-1Thru 16	5,800 lb	1.234
Westinghouse J46 WE-8B (Electronic Controls)	F7U-3 –17-180 F7U-3P—1-12	5,725 lb	1.28
Westinghouse J46 WE-8 (Hydromech,controls)	F7U-3m---1 thru 98	5,725 lb	1.275
Westinghouse J46 WE-18	AZU-1 Thru 96 Cancelled	6,100 lb	

F7U-3
F7U-3M
F7U-3P
A2U-1
  Internal Armament

Effectivity	Guns	Armament Control Systems	
F7U-3	1 to 159	Four 20mm MK12 Guns 720 Rounds Ammunition	Aero 5A Armament Control system (APG-30) Radar-MK6 Mode fire Control MK85 Sight
F7U-3	160 to Sub MK12 Guns 720 Rounds Ammunition	Four 20mm -MK16 Fire Control System –MK 11 Sight Retroactive Incorporation In 17-159	Aero 10 A Armament Control System (APG 30)
F7U-3m	1st and sub MK-12 Guns 720 Rounds Ammunition	Four 20mm Radar –MK16 Fire Control System-MK11 Sight	Aero10 E Armament Control System (APQ-51)
F7U-3P	1 and sub	None	None
A2U-1	1 and sub MK-12 Guns 200 Rounds w/ Space For 360 Rounds	Two 20mm	MK 20 Mod 4 Gunsight

F7U-3
F7U-3M
F7U-3P Pylon Configuration
A2U-1

A2U-1 Tactical Versatility

Item	Fuselage STA No Of Opstai	Store Cssta2	Gross 3	4	5	Cssta6	Opsta7	Stores	Weight	Weight
Rocket PK 32-2.75"	0	0	0	X	0	0	0	1	579	31037
Rocket PK 19-2.75"	X	X	X	X	X	X	X	7	2695	33190
Rocket PK 6A 7-2.75"	X	X	X	X	X	X	X	7	994	31489
Rocket Pk zuni 4-5"	X	X	X	X	X	X	X	7	3360	33855
Bomb 250 lb GP or AAC	X	X	X	X	X	X	X	7	1750	32,245
Bomb 500 lb GP Or Dac	X	X	X	X	X	X	X	7	3500	33995
Bomb 1000 lb	0	X	0	X	0	X	0	3	3000	33501
Bomb 2000 lb	0	X	0	X	0	X	0	2	4000	34404
Bomb 2000 lb	0	X	0	X	0	X	0	3	6000	36501
Bombs 500 lb And 2000 lb	500	2000	0	2000	500	5	7000	37541		
Bombs 500 lb And 2000 lb	500	2000	500	500	500	2000	500	7	6500	36995
Drop Tank	0	X	0	0	0	X	0	2	2204	32608

V-396 Cutlass Missile Carrier

Vought engineers proposed the V-396 cutlass missile carrier on 15 November 1954; it involved the combination of the more ambient design aspects of the F7U-3M and the stillborn A2U-1. The choice component selection and eventual inclusion would provide this new design with Sparrow 1 missile capabilities involving the F7U-3M and the increased fuel capacity once evident in the A2U-1. It is through this union that a significant increase in combat radius would be achieved, along with a slightly higher ceiling and V_{max} over conventional F7U-3Ms then in operation.

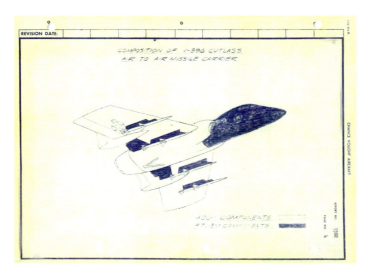

Compositional drawing of Vought's V-396 proposal. It embodied the elements of an F7U-3M forward fuselage forward of fuselage station break 256. Behind this point resides the A2U-1 airframe. *Courtesy Vought Heritage Foundation*

The V-396 consisted mainly of an F7U-3M front fuselage section mated to an A2U-1 aft section consisting of a mid and aft fuselage, wings, and tail. This new design differs to that of the F7U-3M only in ground clearance due to the longer landing gear.

Two hundred and sixty-eight pounds of weight were eliminated while increasing fuel capacity to that of 186 gallons, which increased the V-396's overall range to 94 miles over that of the F7U-3M. The latest A2U-1 design improvements were used, culminating in the following:

A) Allowed an increase in permissible landing weight from 24,000 lb to 25,000 lb
B) Three additional store stations were provided on the fuselage to carry bombs or rocket cutlass.
C) The trend towards the utilization of a simpler control system, pneumatic system, and flight stabilization system were imitated
D) Producing a lighter weight fuselage gageing system
E) A simpler fuel system
F) The capability of utilizing either J46-WE-8 or 18

Airplane Design

The V-396 airframe, in essence, was composed of the A2U-1 aft section behind the production break at station 265. The forward fuselage section beyond station 265 was solely comprised of that of the F7U-3M. Elements of the F7U-3M involving the speed brakes and wing center section trailing edge instillation were employed strictly for balance purposes in this newest design. The front radome was that of the F7U-3M and retained all relevant equipment used in the F7U-3M.

Power Plant

Provisions were made to use either the Westinghouse J 46-WE-8 or WE-18. This required the relocation of the engine control jack shaft in the WE-8 or the installation of a ball joint stiffener for that of the WE-18. In addition, a thrust meter was installed in both engine arrangements.

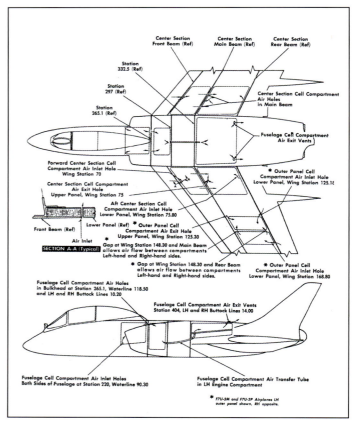

Fuel cell diagram is reticent of what the A2U-1 and V-396 could carry. *Courtesy Author*

144

Fuel System

Internal fuel capacity had been increased to 1756 gallons in comparison to 1570 gallons maintained in the F7U-3M and 1672 gallons garnered in the A2U-1.This was the direct result of the wing center section, and utilizing the space vacated by the removal of the guns and ammunition located in the right and left hand gun bays of the forward fuselage. Fuel was contained in bladder cells throughout the airframe, and especially with self sealing tanks located in the fuselage. Fire suppression was also included in this design, and a fuel management system was installed, providing the transfer of fuel throughout the airframe in order to facilitate and maintain proper aircraft balance in all flight modes.

In the newest inclusion of onboard fuel, as noted in the F7U-3M and A2U-1 designs, provisions had been made in the V-396 proposal to carry additional fuel in externally mounted 150 gallon drop tanks on the center section pylons, or in a 220 gallon reusable fuel pod on the fuselage.

Armament Installation

The V-396 employed all the F7U-3M and A2U-1 armament installations, except the use of guns, which were eliminated.

Four Sparrow 1 air to air missiles were carried on two wing center section and two outer panel pylons. The Sparrow 1 missile is radar operated and homes in on the target through a gun sight in conjunction with the radar beam facilitated by the AN/APQ-51 radar. In addition, this radar supplies range inputs of the target to the MK-16 MOD 4 fire control system.

Consequently, the A2U-1 external stores were maintained, seven store stations in all. The two center section wing pylons could carry up to 3500 lbs of munitions each, while the two outer wing pylons and two fuselage outboard stations could carry a 500 lb bomb each. By removing the APQ 51 radar provision could then be made for the instillation of the labs system.

A Summary of all external store loadings included:

Item sta 117	o.p sta 2,6	c.s fuse-sta. 3	No.of 4	Total Store 5	Store: Rackect Stores	Gross	WJ.	WT	Weight
Sparrow1 Missile	X	X	0	0	0	4	1340	1924	32951
CVA Rocket Pack 32-2.75" Rocket Packs	0	0	0	0	0	1	395	395	31962
FX-6A 7RD 2.75"	X	X	X	X	X	7	994	1387	32414
Rocket Pack Zuni 4-5	X	X	X	X	X	7	3360	3753	34780
Bomb 250"G.P or Dac shape	X	X	X	X	X	7	1750	2143	33170
Bomb 500"G.P Or Dac Shape	X	X	X	X	X	7	3500	3893	34920
Bomb 1000"G.P. Or Dac shape	0	X	0	X	0	3	3000	3399	34426
Bomb 2000"G.P Or Dac Shape Bombs 500"	0	X	0	X	0	3	6000	6399	37426
And 2000"	500	2000	0	2000		3	5	7000	7440	38467

Alighting Gear

The main gear, wheels, and brakes characteristic to that of the A2U-1 were used. This gear was equipped with a 30x7.7 wheel and tire, but was capable of utilizing a 34 x 9.9 wheel and tire, primarily for use on unpaved runways. The braking capacity had been enhanced by 23% in order to cope with the overall increased airframe weight of up to 25,000 lbs.

The main nose gear and wheel/oleo strut are identical for the F7U-3M and A2U-1. Cast magnesium wheels were used in this nose wheel orchestration, supporting the use of tubeless and conventional tires because the V-396 could use larger main gear tires, and a longer A2U-1 arresting gear would be employed.

Electrical System

The V-396 AN/APQ-51 radar was powered by a KVA engine Bleed-Air-Drives Ac Turbo-Generator and resided in the front fuselage section. DC power was supplied by two DC generators, one on each engine.

All electronic installation was identical to that of the F7U-3M, consisting mainly of the AN/APQ/-51 radar, MK-16 fire control system, AN/ARC-27 communications in 6B IFF, and AN/ARN-6ADF.

The V-396 main landing gear is similar to that of F7U-3, 3M, and 3P shown. Larger in overall size, it still maintained Vought's robust and exacting design standards. *Courtesy National Naval Aviation Museum*

The V-396 design embraced essentially the same arrestor gear-hook arrangement as the F7U-3, 3M, and 3P. *Courtesy National Naval Aviation Museum.*

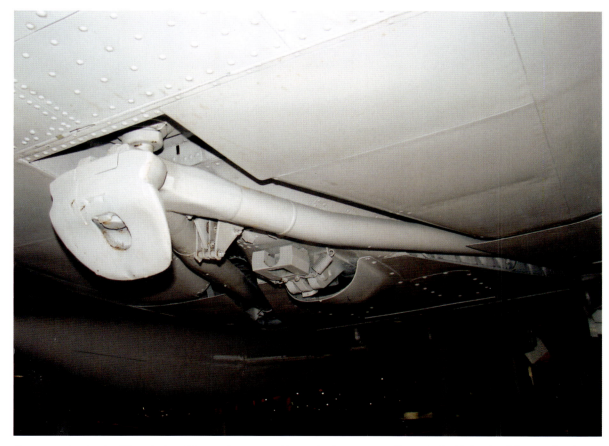

Same arrestor hook, different view. Observe how stout this mechanism appears. Dynamically this hook, while engaging the arrestor cable, had to abruptly stop an aircraft weighing up to 30,000 lbs within 1-2 seconds, traveling at an indicated air speed of at least 118 knots. This inherent loading alone would snap the hardiest of designs. *Courtesy National Naval Aviation Museum*

Cockpit

The cockpit of the V-396 proposed aircraft would consist primarily of that of the F7U-3M, requiring only the slightest of modifications when special weapons were involved in order to accommodate the latter's radar controls; the missile jettisoning panel and external store station and selector were substituted by a special weapons control panel and an alternate external station selector.

Air Conditioning and Oxygen System

The current air conditioning system used in the F7U-3M aircraft was placated for use in the V-396. The only exception would be the included use of a 514 cubic inch oxygen bottle.

Control System

The A2U-1 surface control system was emphasized in the V-396's design features. Improvements to this system would include an overall reduction in weight through the removal of a pump located on each of the tandem systems and the redesigned flight stabilization system. Emergency hydraulic power was supplied in the event of a total system failure through a battery powered electrically driven hydraulic pump.

V396 cockpit was essentially the same as the F7U-3M forward fuselage cockpit tub and retained basically the same equipment. Here the same gun sight is highlighted and undoubtedly would be used as well. *Courtesy National Naval Aviation Museum*

Ejection seat would be the same as the 3M and designed and manufactured solely by Vought. *Courtesy National Naval Aviation Museum*

AFT canopy bulkhead (in black) helps provide the overall structural rigidity of the midsection of the canopy. *Courtesy National Naval Aviation Museum*

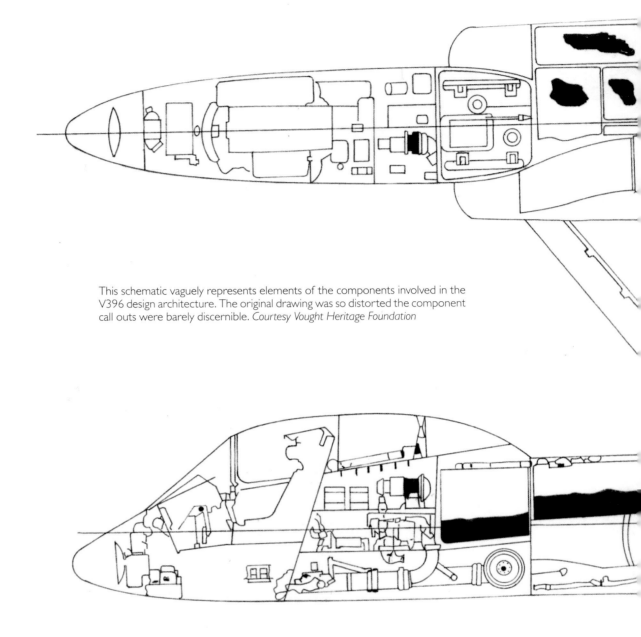

This schematic vaguely represents elements of the components involved in the V396 design architecture. The original drawing was so distorted the component call outs were barely discernible. *Courtesy Vought Heritage Foundation*

The V-396 incorporated the A2U-1 utility hydraulic system. An external hydraulic power receptacle was provided for ground operations.

V-396 Performance Table

	F7U-3m 4 Sparrows 220 Gal	V-396 4 Sparrows 220 Gal	3 Sparrows		
Fuel Pod, Fuel Pod 1-150 Gal Drop Tank					
Engine Based on take-off loading	J46-WE-8	J46-WE-8	J46-WE18	J46-WE-8	J46-WE-8
Gross weight lb	32,968	32,951	32,995	34,681	35,419
Fuel Gal/lb JP4	1570/10,205	1756/11,414	1976/12,844	2126/13,800	
Take-off distance ft	4,630	4,600	4,350	5070	5290

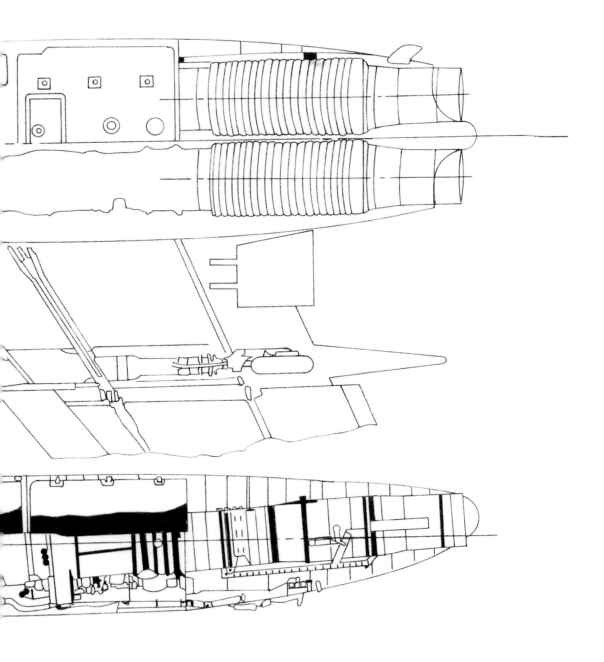

Wind reqd for catapulting					
H8-3500 PSIKTS	37	36	37	42	44
C-11 KTS	0	0	0	10	14
Combat radiusNaltmil	196	290	310	345	395
Cycle TimeHR	1.2	1.8	1.9	2.1	2.4
Based on combat stores/on					
Gross weight 60% fuel lb	28,886	28,385	29,543	29,891	
Max speed sealevel KTS	556	560	567	552	552
Max speed 35,000 ft KTS	507	511	517	502	503
Max r/c sealevel ft/min	8050	8480	10,000	7,510	7,270
Combat ceiling ft	41,500	42,200	45,000	41,400	40,900
Based on landing lading					
Gross weight 25% fuel lb	23,917	23,051	23,095	23,351	23,322
Stalling speed power off	105	104	103	105	105

Notes
Wind requirements for c-11 catapulting are based on catapult end speed data from nav airfac
Combat radius is based on mil-c-5011a general purpose fighter mission.

Weight and Balance
V-396 Basic Weight Derivation

Item	Weight-Pounds		
A2U-1	Weight Change V-396		Weight Empty
4362.7	-94.6(1)		4268.1
Wing Group	757.5	-	757.5
Tail Group	2352.1	3.4(2) ⊠2355.5	
Body Group	1430.8	-	1430.8
Alighting Gear	1083.8	57.7(3)	1141.5
Surface Controls			
Total Structure	(9986.9)	(-33.5)	(9953.4)
Engine	Afterbuners	4339.0	-68.0(4) 4271.0
Air Induction &Exhaust System	168.0	24.0(5)	192.8
Cooling system	9.4	--	9.4
Lubricating System	20.5	---	20.5
Fuel System	1529.6	60.3(6)	1589.9
Engine Controls	51.9	--	51.9
Air Turbine	---	53.4(7)	53.
Total Propulsion Group	(6119.)	(69.7)	(6188.9)
Instruments	136.3	25.9(8)	162.2
Hydraulic Group (Utility)	299.4	---	299.4
Electrical Group	661.0	54.0(7)	715.0
Electronic Group	288.6	622.7(9)	911.3
Armament Group	548.5	-26.8(10)	521.7
Furnishings & Air Conditioning	286.4	31.2(11)	317.6
Auxiliary (Arresting) Gear	150.5	--	150.5
Total Equipment Groups	(2370)	(707.0)	(3077.7)
Total Weight Empty	18476.8	743.2	19229.0
Useful Load			
Pilot	200.0	-	200.0
Fuel –Usable 1672 Gal./1756 Gal. JP-4	10868	546.0 (12)	11414.0
Fuel-Trapped-JP-4	76.0	--	76.0
Oil	30.0	---	30.0
Gun and Gun Mounts (2)	236.5	-236.5(12)	--
Ammunition-200 Rds.	142.2	-142.2(12)	--
Miscellaneous Equipment	63.5	23.7(13)	87.2
Total Useful Load	11616.2	191.0	11807.2
Gross Weight	30093.0	934.2	31027.2

Additional information in the form of recommendations and alterations are provided in a summary

Notes:

(1) removal of the wing extended trailing edge is required for balance purposes.

(2) Substituted the F7U-3M fuselage front section for the A2U-1 front section.

(3) The A2U-1 wind driven emergency power control system is replaced by an

electrically driven emergency power control system .

(4) The J46-WE- engine is used in lieu of the J46-WE-18 engine.

(5) Stainless steel shrouds are required in lieu of titanium shrouds due to use of

J46-WE-8 engines.

(6) Provisions are added for gun and ammunition bay fuel on R/H side.

(7) An air turbine-generator AC electrical system replaces the A2U-1

inverter system.

(8) A fuel flow meter system is installed.

(9) AN/ARN-6 radio compass is used in lieu of the AN/ARN-14 navigation

System,all provisions for AN/APA-89 coder are installed.

(10) All provisions for guns and ammunition are removed and the MK-16

Fire control system is substituted for the MK-20 gun sight and related equipment of A2U-1.

(11) Provisions for an additional oxygen bottle are added, and the F7U-3M air conditioning system is used in lieu of the A2U-1 system to provide cooling for the APQ-51 radar.

(12) Eighty-four gallons of fuel is carried in lieu of guns and ammunition.

(13) An additional oxygen bottle is included.

V-396 Alternate Configuration
Weight Derivation

n%Macpounds	C.G.	Weight
Sparrow Mission		
T.O. Gross Weight-Clean Condition –Wheels Down	13.41	31027.2
Add: 2 C.S. Pylons and Launchers	360.0	
2 O.P Pylons and Launchers	224.1	
4 Sparrows	1340.0	
T.O Gross Weight with 4 sparrows-wheels down	14.06	32951.3
LONG RANGE SPARROW MISSION		
T.O. Gross Weight-Clean Condition –Wheels Down	13.41	31027.2
Add: 2 C.S. Pylons and Launchers	360.0	
2 O.P Pylons and Launchers	224.1	
4 Sparrows	1340.0	
Fuselage Fuel-220 Gal. JF-4	1430.0	
T.O. Gross weight with 4 sparrows and fuel pod –w/d	14.04	34681.3
Maximum Range Sparrow Mission		
T.O. Gross Weight-Clean Condition –Wheels Down	13.4	31027.2
Add: 2 O.P Pylons and Launchers	224.1	
1 C.S. Pylons Launcher	180.0	
1 C.S Pylon, Rack and swaybraces	151.0	
3 Sparrows	1005.0	
1 Drop Tank-150 Gal.	127.0	
1 Fuselage Fuel Pod	300.0	
Drop Tanl Fuel-150 Gal. JP-4	975.0	
Pod Fuel -220 Gal.-JP-4	1430.0	
T.O. Gross Weight with 3 Sparrows and 370 Gal. External Fuel-Wheels Down	13.98	35419.3

Like most of the Vought proposals, the V-396 would eventually find its place in aeronautical obscurity. This design in particular held much promise, ushering in the dawn of missile deployment as an offensive weapons systems for fleet interceptors. Lessons learned later in Vietnam would emphasize and galvanize the need for gun armament on all fighter and fighter-bombers. The Cutlass, in all of its variations, both actual and proposed, spawned the initial crossover from guns to missiles on high performance naval jet aircraft.

Chapter 9

Stall, Spin Testing, and Accidents

"There have been some fifty proven spin accidents within the last two years, with twenty-five fatalities," laments Cmdr. Donald Engen, as chronicled in an article for fleet use on spins. Statistics on spin accidents occurring from aircraft for fleet use, and compiled by the Naval Aviation Safety Center from July 1954 to January 1957, detailed the existence of 70 such accidents.

Excluded from the data would be numerous "stall spin" accidents occurring near the ground during take-offs, wave-offs, or landings. Twelve of these accidents would include trainers. The rest were operational aircraft, comprised mostly of jets. Of these unfortunate airframes, 27% fell victim from offensive maneuvers, 17% from normal flight configurations, 17% from aerobatic posturing, 13% from formation flying, 19% from other various flight attitudes, and lastly 9% were of undetermined origin. Of these 70 documented accidents, 55% resulted in fatalities.

Cmdr. Engen cited "That for each type of airplane there are well established spin, recovery procedures, worked out in the manufacture's spin demonstrations; that the pilot must be familiar with these procedures; and that the pilot must school himself so that when he gets into an inadvertent spin, he will do the right thing-analyze the maneuver to determine just what type of spin he was in, and then apply the appropriate recovery procedure."

Cmdr. Engen finally concluded with this following civet, "above all, remember that your airplane is a weapon with a mission. You cannot afford to compromise the effectiveness of your airplane through ignorance or fear of spins."

Predicated upon the foregoing remarks, the general and prevailing attitudes about spinning or the resolution thereof rests solely upon the pilot. R.F. Sohn summarized this problem in the following statement. "Spins below 28,000 feet made to demonstration specifications (In contemporary fighter aircraft) are practically tantamount to suicide. It is readily apparent that accidental spins, which follow the pattern evidently anticipated in the writing of spin demonstration specifications, will be limited to altitudes above 30,000 feet. If spins are encountered below this altitude, it must be recommended that the pilot eject."

Statistical analysis explicitly demonstrated that the spin, though of no apparent tactical use, is nevertheless a maneuver that must be dealt with. Due to the rapid advance of aerodynamics and its influence on contemporary design trends in the areas of high wing loading, low aspect ratio wings, lengthwise concentration of mass, and marginalizing overall inherent stability, produce aircraft from the design crucible displaying aberrant spin characteristics.

Certain tactical maneuvers unique to that specific aircraft employing high angles of attack at especially lower airspeeds, and thus inviting a spin, would require sufficient altitude for recovery to take place, compromising the maneuvering capabilities of his vehicle. Included in these same design trends, and precipitated by higher speeds and altitudes, were unmanageable spins brought about by other types of uncontrolled motion, specifically directional divergence at high supersonic speeds and roll divergence in inertia coupled rolls. At one end, set at zero angle of attack at maximum angle of attack at low air speed initiated the spin. In between lies the post-stall gyration, the accelerated or high speed spin, and finally the inertia coupled roll.

As with its other contempories, the Cutlass was no exception. The Navy approached Vought with this problem, and aptly applied the flying skills of company test pilot John McGuyrt to this task. On 7 April 1954 McGuyrt experienced a post stall gyration and had to eject, resulting in the loss of his aircraft.

In the following months Don Schultz enlisted efforts on behalf of Vought and would fly more than one-hundred test flights on F7U-3 Bu no. 129566 only to verify wind tunnel results testifying to the aircraft's ability in regaining stable flight without any further pilot inputs during this condition. During this sequestered set of flights an emergency parachute was placed in the vicinity of the tail cone without first encountering structural modifications.

F7U3 BuNo 129566 all white Cutlass was specially prepared for spin testing at Vought. *Courtesy Jay Miller Collection*

No "566" being towed by a mule in preparation for its next test. *Courtesy Vought Heritage Foundation*

Same aircraft pictured with left side boarding ladder and instrumentation boom. *Courtesy Author*

F7U-3 cutlass "556" would later be remanded for further gyration testing at the Cornell Aeronautical Laboratory at the hands of John Seal. The Cutlass was chosen for its unusual blend of aeronautic design and expressed functionality. It would be a model predicating and validating future aircraft designs and flight stabilization systems.

Both theoretical and actual flight tests were initiated, investigating large uncontrolled motions of airplanes as early as 1957, by the flight research department of Cornell Aeronautical Laboratory for the Bureau of Aeronautics. These tests were conducted with the expressed intent of determining their cause and the means of their prevention.

F7U-3 BuNo 129566 view showing "spin chute" installation and jettison mechanism used only in the event of a spin. Attachment structure is quite robust in nature and provided the added strength in the attachment point for the parachute. *Courtesy Jay Miller Collection*

This investigation began with the theoretical study of the post-stall motions of the F7U-3. These uncontrolled motions were simulated by Vought engineers using five-degree-of-freedom equations of motion, which negate speed changes and include only static aerodynamic characteristics based upon damping in roll. Wind tunnel tests performed at the David Taylor model basin 8 by 10 foot subsonic tunnel established static aerodynamic data at high angles at attack.

Flight Test Equipment

Flight test equipment would include the test article F7U-3 Bu. No 129566 fully instrumented with an analog computer, recording instrumentation, and automatic control system. Elements of that system would included the computer, sensors, servo elements, and control surface structure.

F7U-3 No "566" (BuNo 129566) is shown here with the vertical canard used in the "Cornell Study" on post gyration stalls on take off rotation. *Courtesy Jay Miller Collection*

566 with full instrumentation on another test flight. Test results from their specially designed flight stabilization system was a "water shed" event, paving the way for digital flight stabilizing and control systems in use today. *Courtesy Jay Miller Collection*

A vertical canard mounted on the nose of the F7U-3 was the means by which yawing moments could be produced aerodynamically to counter or off-set the onset of a stall.

This vertical canard was comprised of three sections: the upper and lower panels and a center section shaft. Supported by five bearings and a hydraulically operated motor positioned over the torque box, which in turn was attached to a forward fuselage bulkhead. Electro-Hydraulic servos moved this canard upon signal inputs from all corresponding sensors via the analog computer controlled automatic flight system. A pressure limiting device was included in the system for the hydraulic motor, thus limiting control surface hinge moment of the canard and its angle of attack. Discussions of control signal inputs and outputs were governed with pertinent equipment via analog computer and electronic filters whose description is beyond the scope of this text.

Flight Test Results

Taken from section iv, the Cornell University study stipulates the following. "Tests of the F7U-3 airplane in stalled flight were performed, both with and without the canard control surface, in order to determine the efficacy of the automatic control system in preventing large uncontrolled motions of the airplane-post-stall-gyrations." The singular most pressing objective was to obtain flight test results which could be directly correlated to results theoretically predicted on an analog computer.

Conclusions

Through this theoretical and experimental investigation of the control of largely uncontrolled motions of aircraft they successfully completed the objectives. An automatic flight control system designed from purely theoretical constructs was installed in an F7U-3 aircraft and thoroughly flight tested. This control system proved its effectiveness, and especially installed flight-post-stall-gyrations paved the way in its use in high performance aircraft today.

This test proved exceptionally fruitful in its future application and evolutionary nature required for modern day designs. Even though the vertical canard was used quite effectively, the same effect could be achieved in enlarged control surfaces found in the rudders. More importantly, theoretical data derived from wind tunnel tests could be accurately compared to test data, lending greater latitude for the use of theory in future system design.

F7U-3 Accidents

Data compiled by the Navy on the Cutlass spanning from 1952 to 1 March 1957 and predicated on 46,192 hours of flight time revealed some disconcerting discoveries. During this evaluation and fleet indoctrination period 81 major accidents occurred. Out of these 81 incidents 47 are considered strike (reparable), 15 overhaul, and 19 substantially damaged aircraft. Injuries to pilots consisted of 20 fatal, 13 serious, 16 of a minor nature, and 32 unaffected.

Close up view of the vertical canard design to dampen out excessive "yaw" motions experienced during ongoing post stall gyration. *Courtesy Jay Miller Collection*

Another port side view of the fully instrumented "566."

During the formation of the first of the F7U-3 squadrons in 1954, the major accident rate was 8.9 aircraft per 10,000 hours of flight time.

Reaching its zenith some 10 months later at 23.3 aircraft lost per 10,000 hours of flight time broke all existing fleet records. From this heightened state of danger the accident rate would soon regress to that of 11.8 aircraft lost per 10,000 hours of actual flight time and would occur at the time of squadron withdrawal of the Cutlass from fleet service.

Comparison with Other Navy Jets

When comparing the Cutlass to its contemporaries, one must take into consideration the total amount of service hours and the frequency of carrier operations. Table 9-1 reveals accident rates for various Navy jet aircraft employed for squadron use for the fiscal years 1955 and 1956.

Comparative U.S. Naval Aircraft Accident Statistics Period 1 July-30 June 1956

Aircraft	Hours	No.	10,000HRS	No	10,000	Lost		
F7U-3 13.8	22,566	36	16,0	17	7.5	9	4 . 0	
F9F-6,7,8	155,084	10.2	35	2.2	20	1,3	6,3	
FJ-2,3 12.9	94,147	88	9.3	44	4.7	18	1 . 9	
FJ-4 33.3	1,003	1	10.0	1	10.0	-	-	
F4D 80.0	1,725	6	34.8	4	23.2	2	1 1 . 6	
A4D	248	1	40.3	-	-	-	-	-
F11F	59	-	-	-	-	-	-	-
F8U 100	75	291	133	1	133	-	-	
Average 1.8	279 9.1	738	291	10.5	101	3.6	4	9
Total to March 1957								
F7U-3	46,192	81	17.5	47	10.2	20	4.3	
F8U-1	2,097	5	24.9	3	14.9	1	4.9	

Reasons cited for this statistical study stem from the Naval Aviation Safety Centers' interest in uncovering dangerous trends in each aircraft. It must be noted that based on 10,000 flight hours accidents occurring below this bench mark can alter the rate considerably. It must also be noted that only 10-15% of this actual man hour data was actually flown from carrier decks.

Damage inflicted upon the Cutlass in relation to its contemporaries was much greater, and possible reasons would include:

A. Heavier Aircraft
B. Long Nose Gear
C. Higher Performance
D. The Navy's decision not to repair extensively damaged aircraft.

The Cutlass, based on causal factors, would reveal a significant or dominant trend in pilot error, rather than any other error as the imminent cause for accidents. Also revealed statistically, accidents were higher in occurrence with pilots with less than 50 hours of flight in the Cutlass. Out of this statistical milestone, 47% of all Cutlass pilots entertaining 50 hours or less of flight time would be accountable for pilot error induced accidents.

Accidental Factors/Cause and Effect

A. Pilot Error

This category supersedes all others, only to be moderately rivaled by materiel failure as a subsequent cause for accidents. Forty-nine percent of all Cutlass accidents can be directly linked to pilot error. Twenty-six percent of all pilot error included accidents occurred during the landing phase of flight. This would include under shoots, hard landings, wheels up, and ground loops. Eight percent of these incidents would involve in-flight stalls or spins.

B. Other Personnel Error

Maintenance error accounts for roughly 19.3% of all prevailing accidents

C. Material Failure

This mode of failure involves 21.5% of accidents, accentuated by 10.8% attributed to landing gear failure, off set by 6.2% dealing with the fuel lines. Salt air corrosion posed an appreciable problem for the airframe of the Cutlass, but is often glossed over and never addressed.

D. Airport and Carrier Facility

This is probably the smallest category, maintaining only 2.3% of all accidents

E. Undetermined

Of all accidents, 8% are relegated to the unknown. Linked to control problems (stall/spin) or material failure precipitates or compounded by maintenance error.

Accidents by Phase of Flight

The landing phase posed the most appreciable share of accidents, accounting for 46.6%. The in-flight phase accounts for 37.5% and the take-off phase accounts for 15.9%.

Strike damage (structural) is highest in the in-flight phase, weighing in at 85%. Take-off rate is 72%, off-set by the landing phase at 36.5%. Fatality rates per accident are highest at 42% during take-off. The in-flight phase rate is 36%, and the landing phase is lowest at only 9.8%

Ejections

Twenty-two pilots performed the often dreaded ejection maneuver from the Cutlass. Out of these ejections 5 were fatal, 4 warranted serious injuries, 7 were minor, and 6 expressed no ill effects. The 5 fatal ejections all involved some or complete loss of aircraft control experienced below 2,000 feet. Causes for intentional ejections were:

5 Stall/Spin
5 Loss Of Control
5 Fire
4 Main Landing Gear Failure
1 Disorientation
1 Flame Out

Suggested Preventative Action
It was determined that some suggestive action be taken in lieu of progressing events in fact contributing to the nature of the accidents instead of resolving them. The Cutlass would soon be removed from squadron status, only to be superseded by its stable mate, the F8U Crusader.

Conclusions and Pilot Flight Recollections
Bill Montague, a former U.S. Navy fighter pilot, flew the Cutlass and received his initial flight instruction from the late Wally Schirra, who at the time would eventually become one of the "Esteemed" Mercury Seven astronauts. Both revered this aircraft and its flying qualities, which would dismiss or refute the negative image embraced by some pilots during its active deployment.

This "star crossed" Cutlass has seen better days, and was eventually deemed not repairable and relegated to the scrap heap. *Courtesy Tom Cathcart*

Test results proved promising and recommended increasing the vertical rudder surface area to dampen out excessive yawing moments and divergent motions experienced during flight. *Courtesy Author*

F7U-3M BuNo 129663 aboard the USS *Bon Homme Richard* is caught by the crash net to survive another day. *Courtesy Tom Cathcart*

Captain Wally Schirra would not hesitate commenting about the unusual but eloquent flight characteristics of his Cutlass, especially when the slats were extended at low approach and flight speeds; the Cutlass would not stall. If not employed post-stall gyration would occur. Captain Schirra would later reminisce of his experience, especially at high altitude, performing combat maneuvers at low indicated airspeeds at about mach .90 with slats fully extended. He literally could out-turn many contemporary aircraft of the Cutlass while sustaining full afterburner. Schirra further comments on the exceptional stability of the Cutlass with its slats fully deployed during high speed descents from high cone to low cone. Almost vertical recovery was achieved through full afterburning at low altitude of the low cone. Bill Montague would also testify to the fact of how he enjoyed flying the Cutlass at high speeds, performing aerobatic maneuvers especially in the absence of any restriction on g loading.

The late Carl "Tex" Birdwell, obtaining the rank of Captain as a U.S. Naval Aviator, shared his experiences flying the Cutlass at NAS Moffett field through a letter sent to Tom Cathcart at The Flight Restoration Center, Museum of Flight in Seattle, Washington:

"Dear Tom:

Thank you very much for your Cutlass care package of the 8th. Hard to believe there is someone out there just as avid and eager as some of the troops at the Smithsonian (and possibly merry old England) about airplane restoration."

Mr. Cathcart is currently restoring an F7U-3 Cutlass Bu no. 129554 and required some informational assistance from the late captain. Captain Birdwell further recollects:

"In so far as my comments about flying the old 'Gutless,' I can only say that it was great too. My jet experience before getting checked out in the F7U-3, was limited to TV-2 (T-33) and F9F's so at the time I had nothing else to compare with. My first flight was with VE-3, the transition training unit at NAS Moffett. The IP that chased me on the first flight was Wally Schirra. We both would up together at the Naval Air Test Center at Patuxent River later. The procedure in those days was to have a new squadron senior pilots get checked out by the experts first, then filter down the knowledge to the younger lads. First thing was we did some 'approaches' to a stall in various configurations. I noted that old Wally flying tight wing on me right up to break point. Ether he had a lot of gall or extreme confidence!

"The airplane was straight forward in stability and control installed and the G-4 stabilization system operating. As you know, flying wing type of machines are basically unstable in the longitudintion axis and without the artificial stability the F7U was just about un flyable. Like most Vought airplanes, the F7U was no piece of cake stalled out. It had a wicked post stall gyration and fairly difficult spin recovery if allowed to progress that far. The F4U did that, the F8U did it and so did the A-7. Recovery from a post-stall-gyration was to just let go of all controls then fly the airplane out of whatever attitude one would up in. Too many people threw in what they thought was spin recovery control with the result that they really got into a dandy spin. I could say a lot about good flying qualities what most people would F7U didn't have."

Captain Birdwell concludes:

"For its day the performance of the F7U was spectacular (for a short period of time), except for endurance. It would outrun any other machine, including Air Force types like the F86D. We enjoyed many a dog fight with our sister VF-211 with FJ-3s. They cleverly waited until we were almost out of JP-4 before attacking."

Conclusions
"Gutless Cutlass," "Ensign Eliminator," and "Widow Maker" were names endearing in stature that unjustly labeled the Cutlass forever in aviation history. It is apparent that the Cutlass demanded the care and respect of an experienced aviator. This was the pinnacle, cutting edge of aviation and aerospace technology at the time, and would demand the respect of the engineers, production, maintenance, and pilots as well.

There is absolutely no doubt of the Cutlass' truest potential, only to be glimpsed when in full afterburner. The Navy, in all its wisdom, kept changing the Cutlass, subsequently diminishing its performance as such. The under-powered J46 Turbo Jets just added insult to injury.

The inordinately high nose gear, severely restricting the pilot's visibility, and originally designed as a high lift enhancement, was the Achilles heal, and largest cause of accidents. In many respects the Cutlass was a transitional fighter. During its rather protracted developmental period, accented with its abbreviated service life, the fleet carriers changed from World War II Essex type to that of the more modern carriers employing angled flight decks. It also pioneered the use of guided air-to-air missiles for offensive use. For whatever reason, as this "star crossed" fighter would be known, it must be understood that the Cutlass, however remembered, was a necessary weapons program. Developed in a time of rapid and unrelenting expansion of technology, the Cutlass contributed significantly to the aeronautical gene pool and should be recognized as such

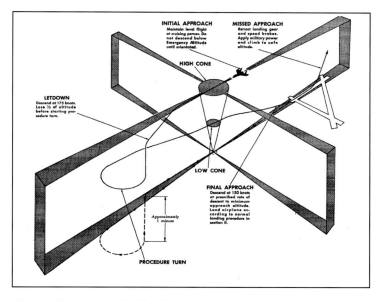

Flight profile maneuver highlighting landing approach from high altitude (high cone) to a rapid descent to low cone and final approach. This maneuver, often practiced by more experienced pilots, if performed properly proved advantageous to all involved. *Courtesy Author*

Chapter 10

F7U-3 Restoration

This chapter deals with the restoration of a F7U-3 Cutlass (Bu No 12 9554) at the Museum of Flight Restoration Center in Everett, Washington. This example belongs to the center's head curator and restorer, Tom Cathcart. The following photos and captioning were graciously provided by Mr. Cathcart, and provide the reader with a more intimate perspective of the compelling complexities synonymous with the aircraft. Much thanks go out to Mr. Cathcart and his skilled team of restoration technicians in the level of detail afforded to this project.

Left engine inlet showing louvers for venting gun gases and open gun bay. *Courtesy Tom Cathcart*

Excellent view showing hunched canopy and downward sloping nose design to improve pilot visibility. Radome housed the APG-30 radar. *Courtesy Tom Cathcart*

Dummy pilot figure shows off a well-practiced maneuver: preparing to pull the face curtain to exit the aircraft. The F7U Cutlass sports a Vought designed seat. *Courtesy Tom Cathcart*

Starboard side engine inlet with access panel open to show routing of hydraulic and electric systems. Dark tinted skins are magnesium. A truly composite aircraft, the F7U employed aluminum, magnesium, fiberglass, wood, steel, and titanium in the fuselage structure and outer wing panels, and some fuselage skins were made of metalite, a Vought term for panels made from sandwiching end grain balsa wood between aluminum sheets to make strong load bearing panels with little internal bracing. *Courtesy Tom Cathcart*

Right lower engine access bay door open showing the location of electronic engine control units. Thrust was regulated by these controls by temperature regulating the afterburner nozzles as the Westinghouse engines were running at 100% RPM at approximately half throttle. *Courtesy Tom Cathcart*

300 gallon Fletcher auxiliary drop tanks were critical to extending the endurance of the F7U-3 beyond about 1.3 hours. Early carrier captains were extremely aggravated by the short time aloft. Internal fuel was carried in nine self sealing bladders, with all fuel dumped to the 184 gallon main engine feed tank before reaching the engines. Leaving the engine in burner could result in running the feed tank empty in a little over a minute if one was not paying attention. *Courtesy Tom Cathcart*

The Westinghouse J46-WE-8B. After lying dormant for 40 years since flying into Spokane, Washington, in May 1957, the two engines were started and run after flushing out the air path and pre-oiling. Both engines starterd to book temperatures and RPM, and all cockpit engine instruments performed as if they were just shut down the day before. *Courtesy Tom Cathcart*

This photo shows the left in board wing trailing edge where the split surface speed brakes reside. The massive surfaces could hold the Cutlass on point in a 80 degree dive, resulting in an extremely stable bombing platform. *Courtesy Tom Cathcart*

A good view of the nose gear wheel well; surely the most complex maze of electrical, hydraulic, and pneumatic systems in the entire aircraft run their course through this compartment. *Courtesy Tom Cathcart*

The infamous nose strut of the F7U-3 at full extension. Tubing with special sliding sleeves ran down the back side of the strut to pipe engine bled air to a set of turbine blades located on the inside of each wheel, thus providing pre-rotation spin up of the nose gear tires in the landing approach to reduce spin up loads and to permit higher airplane sinking speeds. The Cutlass was the first Navy fighter to employ the twin nose wheel arrangement. *Courtesy Tom Cathcart*

The louvers at the upper edge of the engine air inlet is where the pair of Naval gun factory MK12-20mm cannon release their massive destructive power. Early gunnery testing exposed problems with the engines ingesting gun gases, thus producing a compressor stall. Finally understanding the problem, engineers solved these issues through the installation of louvers, vents, and an interrupter system that prevented the guns from firing in unison, which resulted in extreme resonance. When the trigger was depressed two small inlet and outlet doors opened atop the gun bay panel which provided an air path through the gun bay to help eliminate the collection of gun gases. The Aero 10 armament control system and AN/APG-30 ranging radar were intact and functional when the aircraft systems were brought to life in 1997. *Courtesy Tom Cathcart*

The cockpit is still just as it was the day I pulled the Cutlass from the War Memorial Park it resided in for 34 years. The only thing missing is the fire placard that sits just to the left of the turn and bank indicator between four fire warning lights. The gun sight was complete and lit up when the radar system was turned on. *Courtesy Tom Cathcart*

This pilot mannequin strikes a well practiced maneuver that all Cutlass pilots knew by heart. He reaches up to pull the face curtain of the Vought designed ejection seat, which needed at least two thousand feet AGL for a reasonable chance for survival. A spine compressing explosive charge fired after the canopy was released, thus ensuring a discrepancy between one's actual height and that stated in one's drivers license, the seat was positioned by electric motors to the "landing eye" position on approach, giving the pilot an improved vantage point to line up on the numbers. *Courtesy Tom Cathcart*

Another view of the cockpit layout. The T handles to the left of the pilot's knee were to grip when the throttles were placed in full burner, preventing the pilot from inadvertently pulling them back when being catapulted from the carrier. *Courtesy Tom Cathcart*

Looking at the top of the left main gear. What looks like black paint in the gear well is actually black parelketone. For a period of time they sprayed every inch of the landing gear, wells, and exposed areas of the wing fold to attempt to limit corrosion. What they ultimately found was it was hiding corrosion, making it more difficult to detect. This VA 212 aircraft will be restored with the parelketone applied as it was on the 1956 West Pac tour aboard CVA-31. *Courtesy Tom Cathcart*

The Cutlass used huge pitch and roll surfaces called ailevators, as the Brits had already coined the term elevons. Note the thick trailing edge. *Courtesy Tom Cathcart*

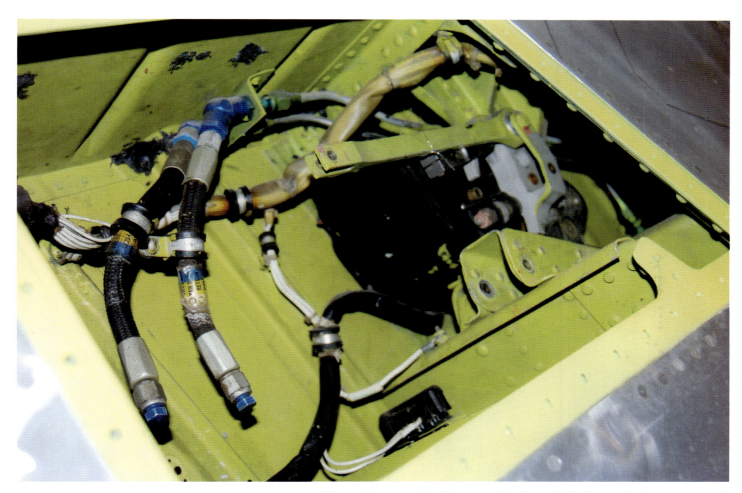

The electric hydraulic servo for the yaw damping system located in the right vertical fin. This operated the lower half of the rudder for both trim and yaw. With a completely irreversible hydraulic system, the only control surface actuated by the pilot was the upper portion of the rudder through push-pull tubes. *Courtesy Tom Cathcart*

The right inboard weapons pylon is shown here. When not carrying a 300 gallon auxiliary fuel tank, this station could be loaded with a 500 lb bomb or a nuclear weapon. Lab bombing runs were practiced in which the F7U would arrive on the deck at great speed, initiate a steep climb and pickling the weapon, then completing the maneuver by pulling up and over with a half roll upright and "high tailing" it out of the area. *Courtesy Tom Cathcart*

Left main landing gear. As with all Vought aircraft, the landing gear was of extremely stout design. The gear door is removed in this photograph, but had an approach light installed within that aided the LSO in determining the angle of the approaching Cutlass. *Courtesy Tom Cathcart*

Appendix I

Enclosure (1) to EM-1140
Page 1

TABULATION OF XF7U-1/F7U-1 REPORTED DEFICIENCIES
WITH CORRECTIVE ACTION AND RELATION TO THE F7U-3

ITEM NO.	REPORT REF.	ITEM	DEFICIENCY	F7U-1 CORRECTIVE ACTION	APPLICABILITY TO F7U-3
1.	(c)	Longitudinal control force and position stability	.Static longitudinal control force and position stability, as indicated by the stick force and stick position required to change airspeed from a given trimmed airspeed with control power on, are unacceptable in configuration P (NRP Climb) and P (NRP Vmax).	The complete redesign of the feel system alleviated this condition which was further improved by the installation of the rate pitch damper.	Lack of flight test to date of mechanical feel system and pitch stabilization make factual comment difficult. Believe this arrangement will be at least as good as F7U-1.
2.	(c)	Longitudinal control with control power on at high air speeds.	Longitudinal control with control power on is unacceptable in configuration CR (Cruise) at all airspeeds above 200 knots and below a true MN of 0.89. From a true MN of 0.89 to 0.92 (Maximum tested) the control force stability becomes increasingly negative while longitudinal control becomes very good.	Redesign of the feel system and incorporating of rate pitch damper corrected this condition.	Mechanical feel system and pitch stabilization expected to be satisfactory in this respect.
3.	(c)	Maneuvering longitudinal stability	Maneuvering longitudunal stability with control power on is unacceptable.	This condition was partially corrected by the redesign of the feel system and finally corrected by programming dynamic pressure with Mach number.	Believe that this condition will be acceptable with mechanical feel system.
4.	(c)	Damping of lateral-directional oscillation	Damping of the lateral-directional oscillation is unacceptable.	Corrected by installation of a rate yaw damper.	Yaw stabilization system expected to make this satisfactory.
5.	(c)	Damping of Short period type rudder oscillation	Damping of the short period type rudder oscillation is unacceptable.	Corrected by installation of larger fins and rate yaw damper.	Vertical Tails on F7U-3 similar to those on F7U-1. Expected to be satisfactory.

Enclosure (1) to EM-1140
Page 2

ITEM NO.	REPORT REF.	ITEM	DEFICIENCY	F7U-1 CORRECTIVE ACTION	APPLICABILITY TO F7U-3
6.	(c)	Directional control force and position stability	Directional control force and position stability in configuration WO (Wave-Off) are <u>unacceptable</u>.	Corrected by installation of larger fins and manually controlled rudders.	Vertical Tails on F7U-3 similar to those on F7U-1. Expected to be satisfactory.
7.	(c)	Aileron effectiveness and rolling velocity	Aileron effectiveness and rolling velocity with control power on are <u>unacceptable</u> in configuration PA (Power Approach).	Corrected by increasing aileron throw and installing larger fins.	Long chord ailavators with throw increased over XF7U-1 and tails similar to F7U-1 expected to be satisfactory.
8.	(c)	Normal Stall Characteristics	Normal stall characteristics with control power on are satisfactory in configurations L (Landing) and G (Glide) but are <u>unacceptable</u> in configuration PA (Power Approach) because the stall warning occurs too close to the stall.	Corrected by installation of clean and landing condition stall detectors and a stick shaker.	Patuxent pilots likely to criticize inadequate stall warning. Artificial stall warning removed by Bureau during weight saving program.
9.	(c)	Accelerated stall characteristics	Accelerated stall characteristics with control power on in configuration CR (Cruise) are <u>unacceptable</u> because no stall warning exists and the rudder exhibits a tendency to overbalance at the stall.	Corrected by installation of stall detectors and stick shaker, larger fins and manually controlled rudders of higher aspect ratio.	Expected not to be as good as F7U-1.
10.	(c)	Speed Brakes	Speed Brakes are <u>unacceptable</u> because of the rudder buffet encountered with the brakes half-open. Tests showed that the speed brakes were very ineffective at approximately 50% of full deflection.	The wing speed brakes were redesigned and fuselage speed brakes added to produce the desired effectiveness without rudder buffet. Various Navy pilots agree that these are very satisfactory.	F7U-3 incorporates wing speed brakes only. These have extended chord and are considered as effective as F7U-1 wing speed brakes alone which is adequate for F7U-3 since speed brakes on F7U-3 are not required to augment control system as is the case in F7U-1 which has manual reversion.
11.	(c)	Slat Operation	Wing slat operation is <u>unacceptable</u> because of the excessive time required for retraction.	Improved until now satisfactory by installation of larger hydraulic lines.	Same as F7U-1.

183

Enclosure (1) to BM-1140
Page 3

ITEM NO.	REPORT REF.	ITEM	DEFICIENCY	F7U-1 CORRECTIVE ACTION	APPLICABILITY TO F7U-3
12.	(c)	Windshield optical qualities	The view through the plexiglas side panels of the pilots windshield is unacceptable because of optical distortion.	Alleviated by closer quality control and selection to tighter standards.	Same as F7U-1.
13.	(c)	Elevator feel system.	The elevator artificial feel sys. is unacceptable because of poor force-versus - deflection characteristics near the neutral position of the cam and the possibility of the roller over-running the end of the cam.	Corrected by the installation of redesigned feel system.	Mechanical feel system should give marked improvement.
14.	(c)	Landing Characteristics	Landing characteristics are satisfactory except for the undesirably low directional control force and control position stability.	Improved by installation of larger fins and manually controlled rudders of higher aspect ratio.	Same as F7U-1
15.	(c)	Ailavator power control system	The longitudinal and lateral power control systems are unsatisfactory because of the tendency of the ailavator boost valves to actuate the ailavators even though the stick does not move.	The redesigned feel system improved the control system overall.	Mechanical feel system expected to result in an overall satisfactory control system.
16.	(c)	Cockpit Arrangement	The cockpit arrangement is undesirable.	F7U-1 cockpit arrangement somewhat improved over XF7U-1 with exception of approach vision which remains outstanding deficiency.	Overall improvement of arrangement and greatly improved vision should make this airplane exceptional in this respect.
17.	(d)	Speed Brakes	Speed Brakes are not effective enough and excessive buffeting has been reported at high Mach Nos. by the contractor. (Unacceptable)	The wing speed brakes were redesigned and fuselage speed brakes added to produce the desired effectiveness. Various Navy pilots agree that these are very satisfactory.	Wing speed brakes only on F7U-3. Have extended chord and considered as effective as F7U-1 wing speed brakes alone, which is adequate since speed brakes on F7U-3 not required to augment control system as in case of F7U-1 which has manual reversion.

Enclosure (1) to EM-1140
Page 4

'EM IO.	REPORT REF.	ITEM	DEFICIENCY	F7U-1 CORRECTIVE ACTION	APPLICABILITY TO F7U-3
18.	(d)	Elevator Force Gradient with Speed (Stick Force/g)	Elevator force gradient with speed slopes in the wrong direction.	Ram air programmed with Mach No. to correct this.	Force gradient with speed will slope slightly in wrong direction with mechanical feel system. Considered necessary compromise to relieve reliability and simplicity.
19.	(d)	Neutral Longitudinal stability about trim	Neutral longitudinal stability exists within plus or minus 5 to 10 knots of trim speed in all configurations tested except PA (<u>Unacceptable</u>).	Close attention to elimination of mechanical slop alleviates this situation, somewhat. Some airplanes superior to others in this respect.	With mechanical feel system this defect does not exist. Close attention to detail design has provided relatively slop free spring struts.
₂0.	(d)	Longitudinal force stability above 0.88 INM.	Longitudinal force instability exists above INM of 0.88 (<u>Unacceptable</u>)	Inherent in the aerodynamic characteristics of the airplane. Alleviated by Mach No. programming of ram air.	The effects of this condition have been markedly reduced by long chord ailavators and mechanical feel system to the extent that the trim change is hardly noticeable to the pilot.
₂1.	(d)	Longitudinal oscillation at INM above 0.9	Longitudinal oscillations occur above INM 0.90 and cannot be damped. (<u>Unacceptable</u>)	Installed rate pitch damper which seems to have eliminated this condition.	Pitch damping provided by stabilization system.
₂2.	(d)	Longitudinal stability at an aft c.g.	Longitudinal force and position stability is too low in NRP climb and NRP V_{max} level flight at an aft c.g. position (<u>Unacceptable</u>)	No corrective action taken. Never formally evaluated at aft end of range. Also dynamic stabilization equipment helps to alleviate this problem.	Aft limit c.g. chosen to give satisfactory static stability although with mechanical feel system static stability will be somewhat weaker over whole speed range.
₂3.	(d)	Performance without afterburners	Performance is unsatisfactory without afterburners. (<u>Unsatisfactory</u>)	J34-WE-42 afterburning engines are being installed. Have attained 0.92 in level flight.	V_{max} with J-35 engines 2-5% lower than estimated for these engines. Being investigated by flight testing and analysis. However, pilots will consider good when compared with F7U-1 without A/B. Performance with J46 with A/B expected to be satisfactory.
₂4.	(d)	Aileron forces at low speeds	Aileron centering forces are too high at low speeds (<u>Unsatisfactory</u>)	Reduced strength of centering spring.	CVA pilots consider characteristics satisfactory with mechanical feel system.

Enclosure (1) to EM-1140
Page 5

ITEM NO.	REPORT REF.	ITEM	DEFICIENCY	F7U-1 CORRECTIVE ACTION	APPLICABILITY TO F7U-3
25.	(d)	Control Power Lever	Control power lever is in a poor location, is similar to the speed brake lever, and has no positive lock. (Unsatisfactory)	Relocated lever to an approved location and incorporated restraining detents in console.	Not applicable
26.	(d)	Fuel Transfer and shut-off switches	Fuel transfer switches and shut-off switches are not labeled (Unsatisfactory).	All switches are appropriately labeled.	Satisfactory
27.	(d)	Location of Switches	Generator, battery, pitot beat and engine de-icing switches are not properly located. (Unsatisfactory)	Switch locations have received Mock-Up Board approval in F7U-1. No further complaint received.	Located in accordance with Mock-Up Board approvals.
28.	(d)	Voltammeters	Voltammeters are not properly located. (Unsatisfactory)	Approved by Mock-up Board. No further complaint received	Located in accordance with Mock-up Board approvals.
29.	(d)	Head Clearance	Insufficient head clearance exists for canopy ejection (jettison). (Unsatisfactory)	No action taken.	Satisfactory - due to greatly improved vision which permits pilot to sit at normal eye level position.
30.	(d)	Warning Lights	Warning lights are too numerous (Unsatisfactory).	Reduced number in F7U-1 as requested by Mock-up Board.	All lights in accordance with Mock-up Board decisions. Several additional instrumentation lights in flight test airplane.
31.	(d)	Lateral-directional oscillation	Lateral-directional oscillation characteristics are not satisfactory when yaw damper is not engaged. (Unsatisfactory)	Yaw damper installed in all F7U-1 airplanes for continuous duty. No other action contemplated.	Yaw damper in stabilization system for continuous duty.
32.	(d)	A/B Light-off time	Excessive delay exists in lighting off afterburners (Unsatisfactory)	Lag is inherent in A/B control system. Little if any improvement can be expected of -42 engine.	Acceleration of larger J-35 engine slower on wave-off than smaller J34 engine. J46 engine A/B thrust will build up faster than XF7U-1 engines.
33.	(d)	Lateral trim creeps	Lateral Trim Creeps (Unsatisfactory)	Corrected by proper rigging of feel cages and installation of synchronizer arrangement.	Expected to be rated satisfactory.

Enclosure (1) to EM-1140
Page 6

ITEM NO.	REPORT REF.	ITEM	DEFICIENCY	F7U-1 CORRECTIVE ACTION	APPLICABILITY TO F7U-3
34.	(d)	Stall Warning	No stall warning exists in any configuration (Unsatisfactory)	Corrected by installation of Safe-Flight stall detectors and stick shaker.	MCR-4 (Bureau approved) eliminated stall warning devices.
35.	(d)	Rudder Buffet in NRP Stall in C/C	Excessive rudder buffet occurs at the stall in the clean configuration at the aft c.g., and normal cruise power (Unsatisfactory)	No action taken. No further complaint received.	Not reported by CVA pilots.
36.	(d)	Boost-off control forces	Control forces with control power off are excessive in the PA configuration (Unsatisfactory).	Spring tab spring rate reduced by 1/2.	Not applicable.
37.	(d)	Vision	View over the nose is restricted in carrier approach (Unsatisfactory)	No action taken on F7U-1. Acceptable proposals were made for F7U-2 prior to cancellation of that contract.	MCR-8 Improved Vision nose insures adequacy of approach vision in every conceivable condition.
38.	(d)	Ground Clearance	Maximum angle of attack cannot be obtained on the ground due to insufficient clearance of the vertical fins. (Unsatisfactory)	No change in ground clearance for take-off was made. However, the installation of a nose gear extender for catapulting provided the proper catapulting attitude without necessity for excessive change in attitude after leaving catapult.	Increased ground clearance by cutting down on fin stubs. Method of catapulting (Configuration II) assures adequate ground clearance.
39.	(d)	Shift of control power-off to power on	Shift of control from control power on to off is not satisfactory and should be investigated at all speeds. (Unsatisfactory)	Design changes incorporated in airplane make this system satisfactory. Demonstrated to MN .98.	Not applicable
40.	(d)	Control Stick Length	The control stick is approximately 4 inches too short.	The stick was lengthened 4 inches.	Length set by Mock-Up Board. CVA pilots consider satisfactory.
41.	(d)	Lateral trim switch	Location of the lateral trim tab switch is unsatisfactory.	Location established by Mock-up Board. No further complaints received.	Lateral trim switch on control stick grip. Considered satisfactory.

187

Enclosure (1) to EM-1140
Page 7

ITEM NO.	REPORT REF.	ITEM	DEFICIENCY	F7U-1 CORRECTIVE ACTION	APPLICABILITY TO F7U-3
42.	(d)	Emergency Hydraulic Pump	The endurance of the emergency hydraulic pump (for emergency aileron control) is insufficient and its capacity is marginal.	The 1/4 gpm intermittent duty pump was replaced with a 1/2 gpm continuous duty pump.	Not applicable.
43.	(d)	The Fuel Quantity Gages	The fuel quantity gages for the main fuel and transfer fuel systems are inaccurate.	Currently making trial installation of an improved gaging system which incorporates attitude and density compensation. Kits will be furnished for all F7U-1 airplanes.	Current F7U-3 design better than F7U-1 originally but further improvement necessary for attitude correction and is being designed.
44.	(f)	Vision	Unacceptable and unsatisfactory - The pilot can not see the carrier during the final stages of a normal carrier approach.	No corrective action.	MCR-8 Vision improvement insures satisfactory vision.
45.	(f)	Sinking Speed	Unacceptable and unsatisfactory. It is difficult to consistently obtain impact sinking speeds below design limits in shipboard landings.	No corrective action.	Expected that good approach vision will help alleviate this condition.
46.	(f)	Nose-wheel cocking	The tendency of the nose wheel to become cocked in flight is an unsatisfactory condition.	Design has been released to correct this. Will be incorporated retroactively on a rotation basis.	Internal centering cams in nose gear oleo assures centering in flight.
47.	(f)	Rain in the airspeed system.	Recommended that the effect of rain on the airspeed indications of this model be investigated and that this discrepancy be corrected.	None yet. Possible that addition of a drain hole in pitot head at low point considering extreme attitude of airplane in carrier approach will suffice. Being investigated.	F7U-3 should be investigated and corrective action taken.
48.	(g)	Cross wind take-offs	Rudder control effectiveness in a crosswind take-off is unsatisfactory.	None	Probably worse on F7U-3

Enclosure (1) to EM-1140
Page 8

CY	F7U-1 CORRECTIVE ACTION	APPLICABILITY TO F7U-3
ty of the ear neutral with strong auses over akes pre- ficult. unsatisfac-	None	Mechanical feel system expected to be satisfactory.
racteristics ry. It is e small ateral trim ensitivity ontrol system.	None	Suitable trim actuators employed. Should be satisfactory particularly in conjunction with mechanical feel system.
switch loca- ient.	None	Located on top of stick. Satisfactory.

ITEM NO.	REPORT REF.	ITEM	DEFICIE
49.	(g)	Lateral control sensitivity	The sensitiv lateral control position couplec stick centering controlling and cision flying di This condition tory.
50.	(g)	Lateral trim sensitivity	Lateral trim ch are unsatisfact difficult to ma adjustments in because of the of the lateral
51.	(g)	Lateral trim switch location	The lateral tri tion is inconve

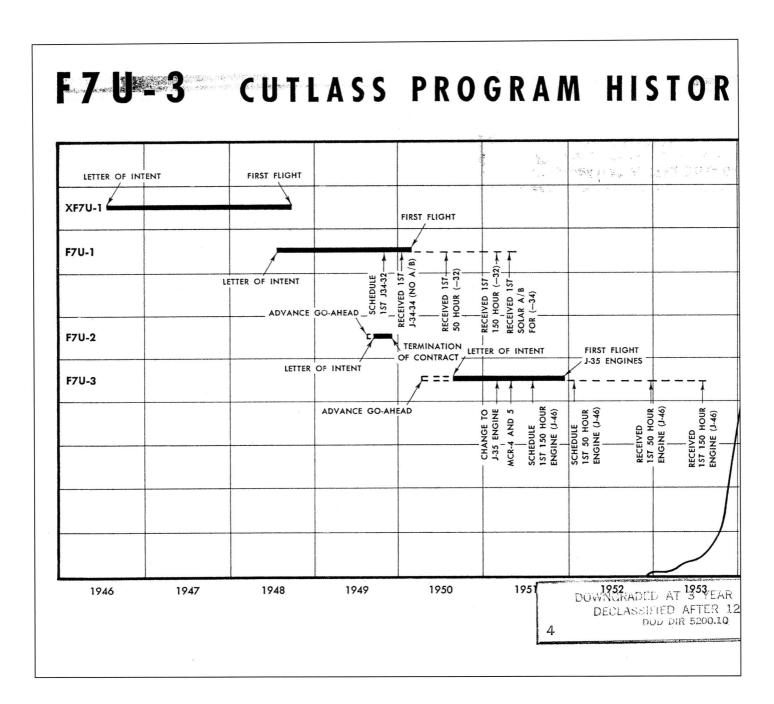

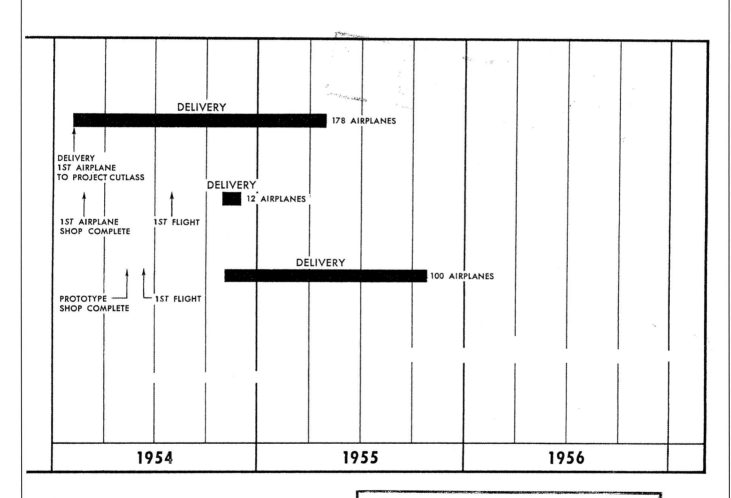

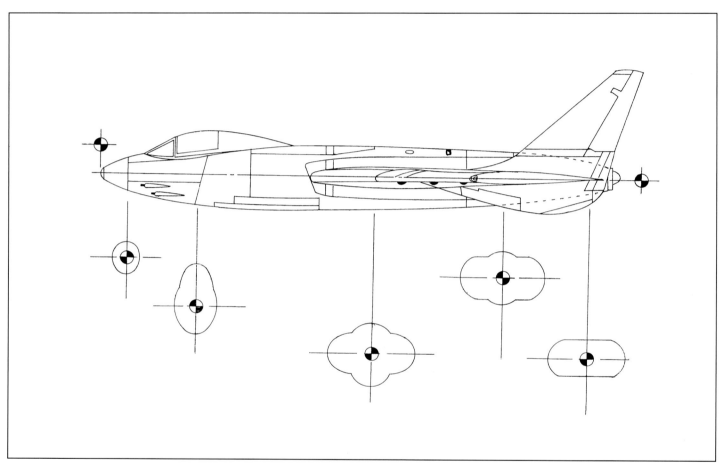

Port side view F7U-1 Cutlass sections 1/72 scale. *Courtesy Author*

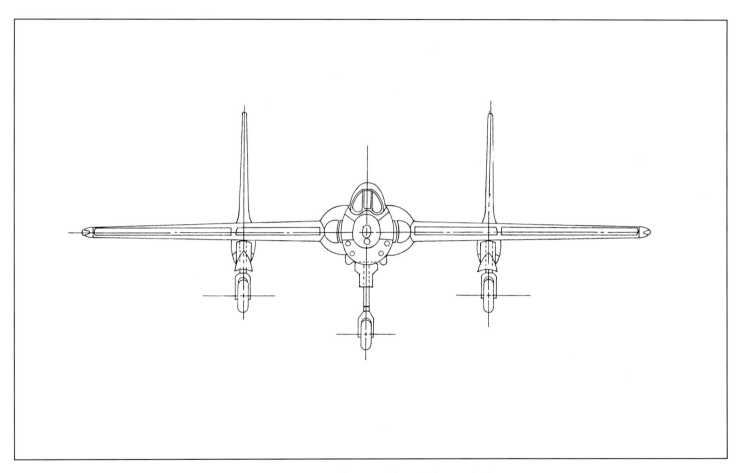

Front view of F7U-1 Cutlass, 1/72 scale. *Courtesy Author*

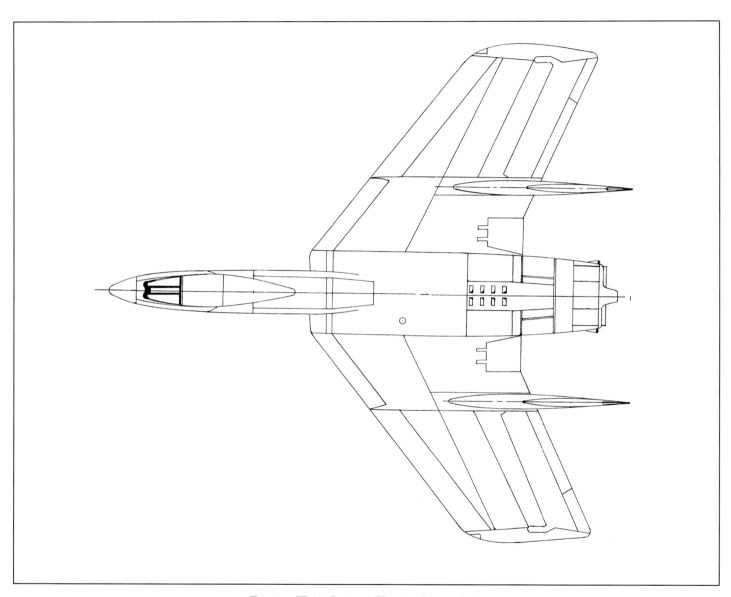

Top view F7U-1 Cutlass, 1/72 scale. *Courtesy Author*

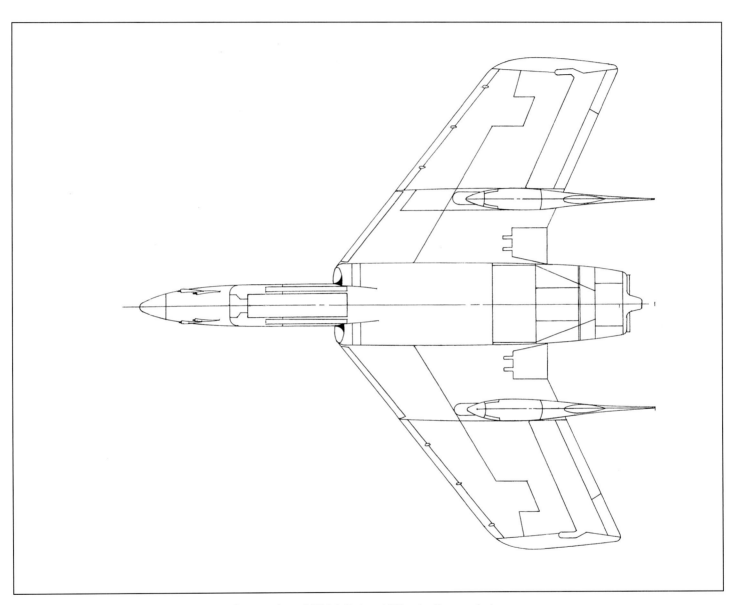

Bottom view of F7U-1 Cutlass, 1/72 scale. *Courtesy Author*

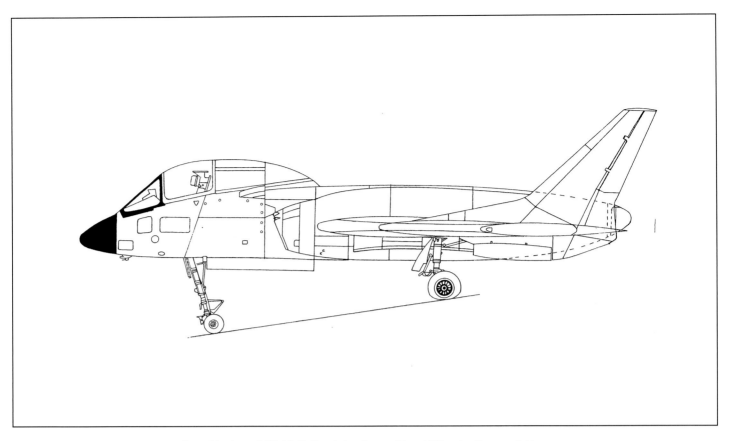
Port side view of F7U-3 Cutlass in landing position, 1/72 scale. *Courtesy Author*

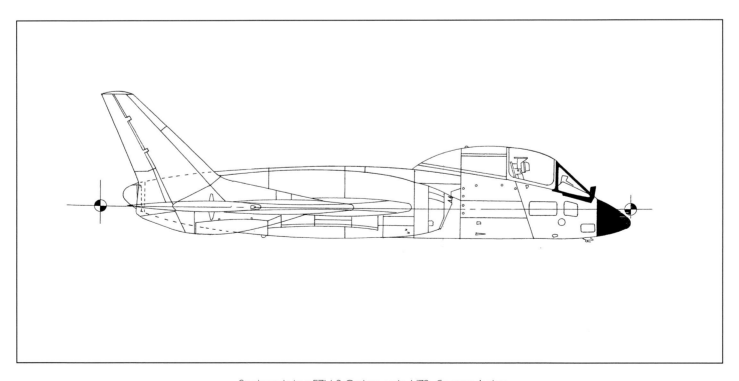
Starboard view F7U-3 Cutlass, scale 1/72. *Courtesy Author*

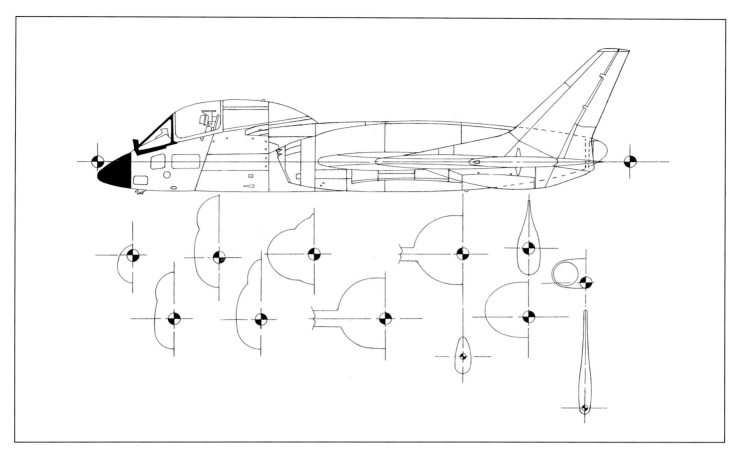

Port side view of F7U-3 Cutlass with fuselage cross section, scale 1/72. *Courtesy Author*

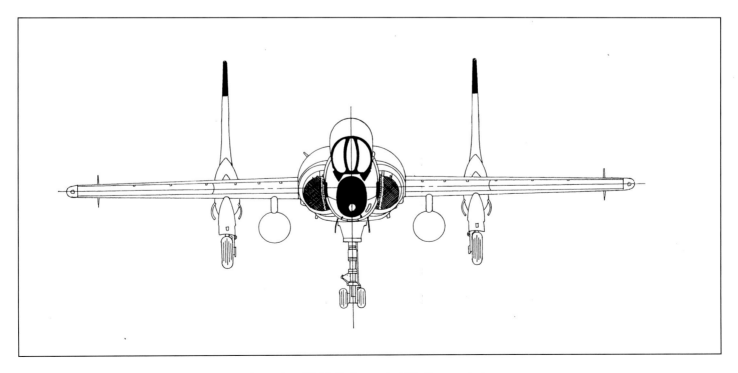

Front view F7U-3 Cutlass, scale 1/72. *Courtesy Author*

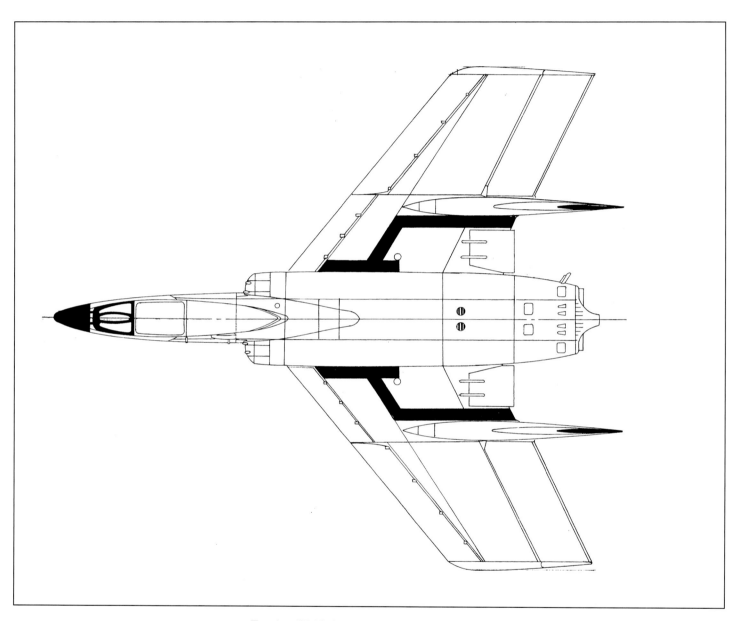

Top view F7U-3 Cutlass, scale 1/72. *Courtesy Author*

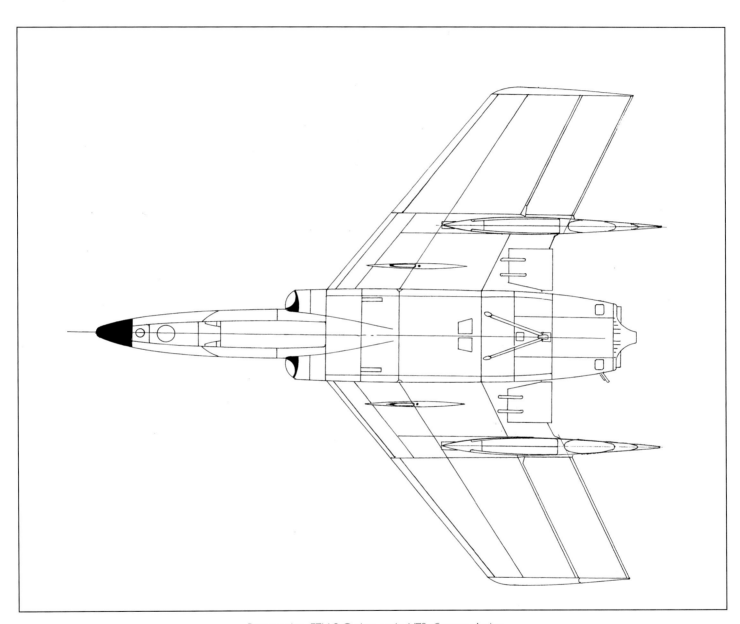

Bottom view F7U-3 Cutlass, scale 1/72. *Courtesy Author*

Bibliography

Abzug ,Malcolm, J., Larrabee, E. Eugene.
Airplane Stability and Control. New York: Chambridge University Press., 2002

Chance Vought F7U-3 Cutlass Pilot's Flight Operating Instructions;reprinted by Periscope Film.com

Chance Vought F7U-3 Structural Manual: US Navy: 1950

Chance Vought F7U-3 Maintenance Manuals: US Navy: 1953,1955, and 1957.

Friedman, Norman, U.S. Aircraft Carriers a Illustrated Design History; Annapolis Maryland: Naval Institute press., 1983

Ginter, Steve, Chance Vought F7U Cutlass: Naval fighters Number Six: Steve Ginter 1982

Moran, Gerald, P. Aeroplanes Vought,1917-1977. Temple City, California : Histroical Aviation Album. 197.

Museum of Flight Restoration Center; VIA Tom Cathcart Cornal University Study "Flight, Stabilization and Control F7U-3" Pub. 1957

Naval Air Technical training command. Aircraft structures. Honolulu, Hawaii: University Press of the Pacific, 1952

Whitford, Ray. Fundamentals of Fighter Design, Shrewbury, SY3 9EB England: Airlife Publishing LTD.,2000

Flight test reports and Standard Aircraft Characteristics ,Patuxent River Naval Air Museum. Patuxent River, Maryland: 1951, 1952, 1953, and 1954

Chance Vought official company documents and records provided by THE Vought Heritage Foundation.

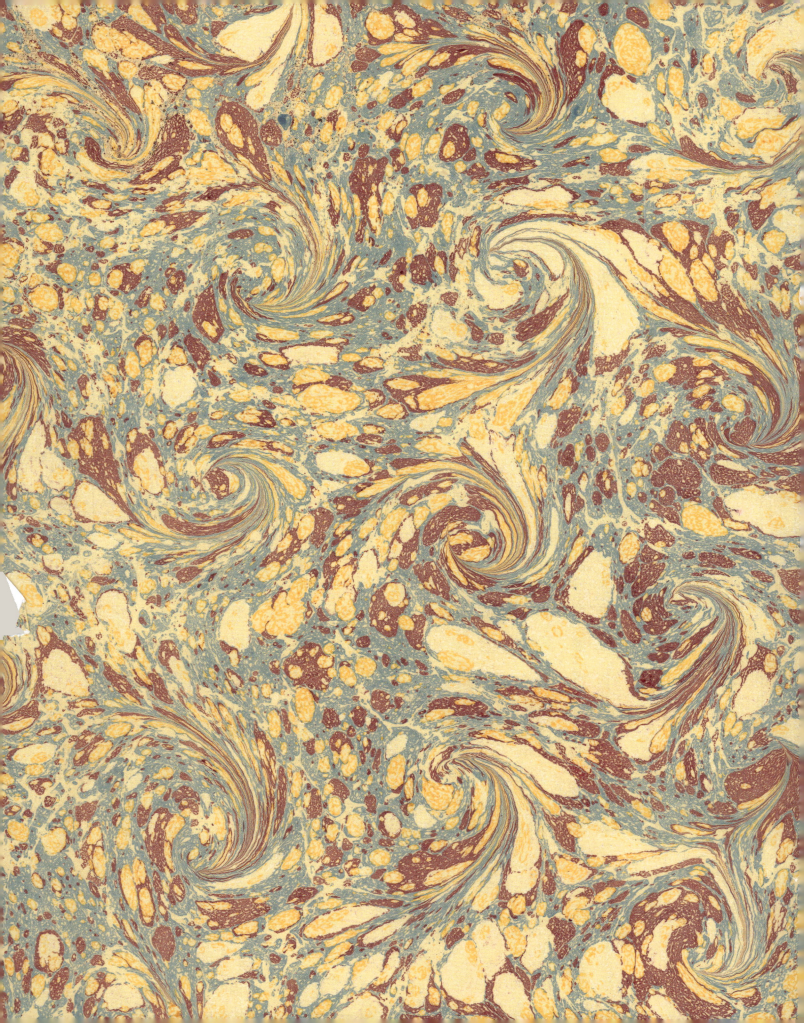